The Liberated Baby Boomer

Making *S P A C E* for Life

An Eclectic Journey
Through Clutter and Beyond

Kater Leatherman

Cover design by Kater Leatherman

Cover image by Aleksandar Velasevic

All photographs in this book are from the author's collection

Author photograph on back cover by Karen Guay

Kiwi Publishing
Fourth Printing, September 2012
ISBN: 0-9876136-1-9

Note: This book is written as a source of information, not a substitute for professional advice.

Also by Kater Leatherman

Making Peace With Your Stuff

. . . because you probably WON'T need it someday

To order Kater's books, go to
www.katerleatherman.com

To contact Kater, email
katerleatherman@gmail.com

To my grandmother,
Marnie,
with deepest gratitude

Acknowledgments

I would like to shine my light on the following people:

Gussie Scardina, my editor. Thank you for finally convincing me that there is no apostrophe in the word "its" and that a period goes inside a quote. Also, to Sandy Patterson for polishing the final draft.

Candace Nikiforou, who formatted this book. You are truly a gift to work with, and as any author knows, I couldn't have birthed this book without you.

My parents, Joan and Gordon Leatherman, for bringing me life – especially in the month of Scorpio!

Kristan Leatherman for her memory, long-distance moral support, and insights.

Kerry Dunnington, who has led the way in the publishing world with her book, *This Book Cooks*.

Dr. Charles Peters for holding me steady when I wanted to run in the face of conflict.

To my friends and acquaintances for their love, understanding, and guidance.

Terry Schaefer. Thank you for holding the *s p a c e* for me to write this book.

AUTHOR'S NOTES

Out of respect for the privacy of others, I have
changed some of the names in this book.

*It is with humility that I write
what I most need to learn.*

Everything that has an ending has a new beginning.
Make peace with that and all will be well.

— from the teachings of Buddha

INTRODUCTION -
A NEW BEGINNING

Let me tell you how I came to write this book.

In September of 1997, I had an epiphany on the way to the grocery store. Just when my blue Subaru Outback turned the corner into the parking lot, I heard three simple words. "Write a book," the small, still voice inside of me said. And so it happened, just as it was supposed to, because I have fallen in love with writing.

Ten years before, I stopped drinking and came to believe that the root cause of my problems ultimately came down to one thing - clutter. And I'm not just talking about material clutter. I am also talking about the internal stuff - emotional, mental, physical, spiritual, visual and verbal. Ultimately, for me, the road to liberation began by acknowledging this.

Clutter begins as a symptom to an underlying problem and how out of balance we are depends on heredity, the amount of negative conditioning we received, and the severity of our wounding. I was 36 years old when I decided to do whatever it took to get unstuck and move on in my life.

Everyone has segments of their history that they don't want to remember. Numbing out becomes a way to cope because it's easier than following the unresolved threads to their source. This is a journey that requires honestly, courage, and commitment.

Even though this book is filled with ways to embrace the truth about clutter, I would like to suggest starting with the Universal Law of Intention. The circumstances of our lives are less about luck and more about the power of intention. By declaring what you want, the Universe will then know how to support you.

You can also begin to address your trigger reactions as they come up in present time. This is the body's natural way of purging clutter. Otherwise, you will eventually manifest some form of dis-ease in the body, mind, and spirit because the body doesn't thrive in clutter's toxic, dark energy.

The most obvious form of clutter comes from our possessions. Here, I'm not talking about deprivation, being a hermit, self-denial, or feeling bored. Simplicity is heart driven, a byproduct of letting go of things that no longer serve you, keep you indebted to others, or take up valuable *s p a c e*. I have included three articles that will guide you through this process - *Fear, Layers of Clutter*, and *Staying Rid of Material Clutter*.

Depending on what you eat, your diet can be classified as cluttered, too. So many of us have ventured away from eating foods in their natural state that it's no wonder we feel tired and sick. To create the *s p a c e* necessary to reawaken your taste buds for real, "living" foods, read *Detox Your Kitchen*. It will help you begin the transition from eating less refined junk to consuming more whole foods.

For addressing physical clutter, yoga is one way to attract more balance into your life. Focused breathing, stretching, and strengthening will clear away mental chatter, physical stress, and emotional tension. With regular practice, your body will open up, release stored memories, and move energy. In *Anusara Yoga*, you will read how this oldest form of self-care is not only a great metaphor for life, but can also bring you back to one of the sweetest *s p a c e s* of all - your natural state of being.

Additional articles include *Tolerations*, i.e., people, places, situations, and things that we put up with on a daily basis that siphon our energy. *Relationships* targets the five different kinds of people and how to balance them in your life. *Verbal* and *Visual Clutter* will raise your awareness and the subtle impact that they have on your life.

While photographs and quotes are added for enjoyment, depth, and inspiration, the heart and soul of this book lies within its stories. For years, I lived in denial and, until I faced the truth about myself, I would never be able to experience emotional freedom, recognize my true potential, and live an authentic life.

One chapter addresses an unusual phobia that I ignored for over 40 years until there was no *s p a c e* left to hide. *Deben* is the story about an African American healer who finally got me out of my head and into my heart. And, in *Anna*, I share the pain associated with learning one of life's most important lessons.

Finally, as a nostalgic baby boomer, I couldn't have written this book without sharing a few of my experiences from the Sixties. There is no other time I would have rather been born into than the one that changed the world. Back then, my generation made things happen because we believed that anything was possible. Yes, we opened up a lot of *s p a c e* as you will read in *Balance*, *Grateful Dead*, and *Y E S*.

I believe that our spiritual work is learning how to live more fully in the present moment. This requires a clear, balanced body, mind, and spirit. The Truth, capital "T," is that everything we think, say, do, feel, and believe creates our reality whether we're paying attention or not. The more you empty the vessel of toxic clutter - no matter how insignificant it may seem - the more you are clearing the *s p a c e* for something new, better, and different to come into your life.

So, wherever you are on your path, may your life be liberated with abundance, health, joy, love, unlimited possibilities, and lots of *s p a c e* for change!

Namaste,

Kater Leatherman

*Sometimes a person has to go back, really back –
to have a sense, an understanding of all that's gone to
make them - before they can go forward.*

– Paule Mardhal

Pour it out. Dump it out. Throw it out.
Empty every bag, box, and bureau. Empty every
closet, every corner, every cupboard, every cell.
Pull it out. Drag it out. Clean it out. Clear it out.
Spread it out, sort it out. Look at what you've
collected, what you've stored, what you carry
around with you every day of your life. Empty out
the old, the unwanted, the unusable. Empty out
the pain, the heartache, the memories. Empty
everything that offers nothing. Leave things empty
for a while. Feel empty. Feel the lack. Feel your
way through the nothingness, until at least
you feel ready to fill again.

– Rachel Snyder

CONTENTS
(in alphabetical order)

In the end these things matter most:
How well did you love? How fully did you live?
How deeply did you learn to let go?

— from the teachings of the Buddha

ANNA

I am sitting cross-legged against the wall in our den, a mountain of unopened boxes staring at me. Outside, the stillness of Otter Pond with its layer of earth-colored leaves skimming the surface is a lovely distraction. However, there is much work to be done, having just moved back into our newly renovated glass house. With my intention in place, I know that by the end of the day, our collection of books, DVDs, framed pictures, and photo albums will be strategically placed on the white, IKEA bookshelves. What I don't know is that there is a trigger reaction lurking inside of me.

Midway through the morning, I decide to take a break and open one of my photo albums, a 12" x 12" book bound in denim blue canvas. Randomly, I open it to the third page. There I am, a chubby ash blonde cherub with sloe eyes and one ear sticking out (see p. 317). Oddly, I first laid eyes on this picture as an adult while rummaging through a box of memorabilia that my mother saved for me.

I turn the album page, which is made of acid-free paper and covered with a clear plastic page protector. There, in black and white, is a photograph of my mother and father - beautiful and handsome, respectively - taken sometime in the early fifties. Clearly, their love for each other looks vibrant and new, before my father's alcoholism strained their marriage and bankrupted his health. Mother has accessorized herself in a mink stole, white hat, and elbow length gloves. Dad is wearing a dark suit, probably navy blue, with a white shirt and striped tie.

On the opposite page is our family Christmas card for 1955. I know the photograph well - a candid shot of my older brother flopped over our black cocker spaniel, Kippy. With the fireplace as a backdrop, he is looking up at my younger sister who is sitting in her wooden rocking chair. I, too, am looking at her, but with a subtle glare in my eyes. I now know why. After she was born, my father's attention and affection shifted from me to her.

I notice that my breathing is shallow and I am feeling anxious and tense, just like the day I returned to visit my childhood home after 30 years. Each step, as I moved from room to room - or now as I turn each album page - might trigger something in me that I don't want to remember.

I turn the page where a Mother's Day card that I made in first grade features two flowers with a yellow sun and some sky and a patch of green grass on the front. Inside, I wrote a poem, only misspelling one word:

Today is Mothers Day.
That is why we are gay.
We would like to say.
We love you evey day.

Clearly, I am on a trip through another lifetime. To drive this point home, the same album page features an invitation to a classmate's birthday party dated April 26, 1958. At the bottom of the card is her telephone number: DR7-9480.

My eyes move to the right, where I see a collage of geeky-looking baby boomers smiling awkwardly for a 1959 class photo. All of us have teeth that are missing, protruding, or *s p a c e d* too far apart. The girls are wearing dresses with Peter Pan collars; the boys have crew cuts. Two of them have slicked their hair so that it is sticking straight up in the front. Under the picture I have written their names - Peggy, Dottie, Ridgie, Dick.

I turn another page.

Immediately, the photograph evokes an emotional response. I swallow hard and sit idle. There, pictured in my parents' living room surrounded by the Steinway piano, French doors, and custom-made draperies is a humble woman, plain and unassuming, who looks wise beyond her years. She is seated, with skin the color of the mahogany piano bench beneath her.

In small print, just below the only picture I have of her, I wrote: "Anna Brown, who worked for my family from 1959-1969."

I close my eyes and squeeze them tight. What a stingy one-liner for a woman who meant so much to me. In an attempt to block out her memory, I keep my eyes closed, but she is still there, a silhouette against the backdrop of my mind. I open my eyes and attempt to soften the growing lump in my throat.

During an outpatient alcohol rehab program, I remember our group counselor talking to us about emotional pain.

"Painful memories don't just go away because we want them to," Jack said, peeling the wrapper off of a piece of hard candy. "They hang out, just waiting for some person, place, or thing to grab your attention."

Jack was a welcome distraction – tall and boyishly attractive with a lopsided grin. He appeared to be in his early thirties, wearing a T-shirt, khaki cargo pants, and red sneakers. I would later find out that he lived in the apartment building directly behind me, intensifying my schoolgirl crush.

"Look, if you are triggered by something, or if you find yourself reacting instead of responding, then that's your cue that something is going on inside. Every time you got too close to the pain, you reached for a drink or drug."

There were seven of us in the group, all newly clean and sober, all anxiously waiting for the fog to lift.

"Eventually, there are going to be consequences if you choose to avoid the pain," Jack said, sucking on his candy.

I thought to myself, *emotional clutter.*

Jack had been where we were and understood.

"I hate to be the one to rock your world, but the way out is the way in. In order to heal your wounds, you must go through the feelings, not around them. Going around them has gotten you here. You've been avoiding the pink elephant in the living room for years."

He paused to tighten the shoelace on his left sneaker, crushing the piece of candy with his teeth.

"When those triggers rear up, you are being asked to remember something. That's where the freedom lies, in choosing to remember. Otherwise, you will continue to manifest what you don't want in your life. You can't move on with stuck energy running through your veins."

I knew that the ability to deny and suppress my emotions protected me. But I didn't see trigger reactions as blessings, that they could actually support my healing. I always tried to make the pain go away with alcohol, drugs, or sleep. Of course, it worked, but for only as long as I was medicated.

I've had this photograph of Anna for years, yet for some reason seeing it today has ignited in me a profound sense of sadness. This must be one of those trigger reactions that Jack was talking about.

I close my eyes again, but neither the picture of her nor the tightness in my throat will go away. My awareness shifts to the memory of our family vacation in the summer of 1960 when we were turned away from a restaurant because Anna was with us.

My stomach wrenches, just like the day that I went cliff jumping, standing at the edge deciding whether to go or stay. I look at the photograph of Anna, her eyes focused softly on me with a look of love and reassurance on her face. My heart is

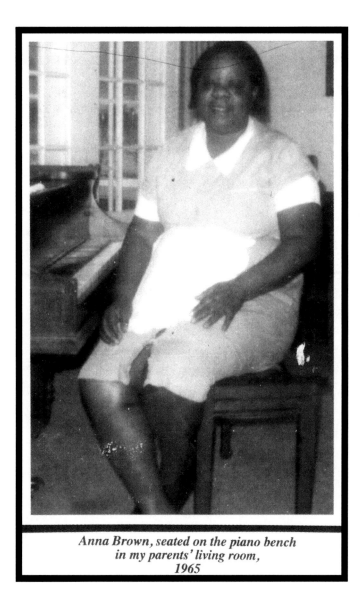

Anna Brown, seated on the piano bench in my parents' living room, 1965

pounding and I feel sick to my stomach. The lump in my throat, like a cork on a champagne bottle, is holding everything inside. The phone rings. I remain still, closing my eyes again. Then, just when the answering machine picks up the call, my insides erupt like a volcano, spilling an uncontrollable rush of warm, salty tears onto my lap.

. . . .

The only memory I have of Anna's first day was my two-year-old brother tumbling down the stairs in his excitement to see her. According to my mother, Anna had worked for a neighbor who never forgave my family when she came to work for us. However, from the time I was eight years old until I turned eighteen, Anna was our domestic goddess, trusted caregiver, and spiritual angel.

The photograph, in muted color, is vintage 1960s. Anna's hair is short, and looks like black straw. It reminds me of hair that children draw on stick figures - stiff and straight - except that hers is combed back behind her ears. At 5'6" and 190 pounds, she is strong and stocky looking.

Her salary in those days was roughly $45.00 for five, twelve-hour workdays. Every weekday morning at 7:00, she would enter through our front door like a breath of fresh air. Then, without dawdling, she would head downstairs to the basement laundry room to change into her work clothes.

Her uniforms came from Hutzlers, the grand dame of department stores in Baltimore at the time. On the second floor, all the way in the back, was a small department for "domestic help" that sported shelves lined with neatly folded uniforms in gray, black, or white.

While I watched in silence from the sidelines, Mother would pick the same style for Anna, just like the uniform in the photograph - a light gray dress with a white collar and short sleeve cuffs. A cotton apron, in white, would complete the ensemble. Then she would hand the sales clerk her metal "shopping plate" with the red leather cover, ask to have it delivered, and off we would go.

Meanwhile, back home, Anna was busy with a schedule that rarely wavered. Monday was laundry day and, with seven of us, it took her all day. On Tuesdays, she ironed what she had washed the day before. The rest of the week - Wednesday, Thursday, and Friday - were her days to clean, polish silver, and do whatever else needed to be done.

In the photograph, although her feet are cropped out, I know what she is wearing: black "Chinese" type slippers. They are thin soled with one torn seam and a hole in the left big toe. Unfortunately, I never remember her wearing anything else.

Throughout the week, she toiled quietly around the house in those black slippers, the sound of daytime soap operas - or "stories" as she called them - humming in the background. Then, sometime around 5:00, she would gather up my younger brother and sister to give them their daily bath.

With less than two hours left in her workday, Anna would make her way into the kitchen to help my mother with dinner. Sometimes, though not often enough, she cooked her specialty - chicken fried in Crisco. When 7:00 p.m. rolled around, she would slip through the breakfast room door where her ride was waiting at the bottom of the driveway.

Anna had no children of her own. She lived with her common law husband who drifted in and out of her life like a rolling stone. As a child, she was raised on a farm with 13 brothers and sisters. One day, I watched her pluck a piece of straw from the kitchen broom and thread it through her pierced ear.

"I don't want the hole to close up, honey," she would tell me when I asked her about it. Now, I wonder if that piece of straw reminded her of those days gone by on that farm.

In the picture, the bottom button is missing on her uniform, creating a slit in the front of her dress. I remember her knee-high stockings being twisted, strangling her trunk-like calves. Still, she manages a soft smile for the camera, and the memory of her sunny disposition and infectious laugh generates more crippling sadness in me.

As she got older and her physical stamina began to wane, I would scurry around the house to help lighten her load. Together, we would accomplish her work in half the time and then watch television for the rest of the day. Of course, we only did this on those rare days when neither one of my parents was home.

Then, in the summer of 1969, on a hot, lazy Monday morning in early June, Anna didn't show up for work.

"She took a job in a Venetian blind factory to make more money," Mother said conversationally when I walked through the kitchen door.

Still hungover from the night before, I turned around, ascended the stairs and crawled back into bed. Then, twisting and turning in the sheets, I tried to make sense out of it. Anna was like a member of our family. If she needed more money, why didn't my parents just give her a raise. I knew that she wouldn't have left us unless something happened.

That summer, which I have since dubbed the Summer of Loss, my high school sweetheart broke up with me, I got drunk the night Neil Armstrong's first historic steps on the moon were televised live, and I missed out on Woodstock. And now Anna was gone. There was no going away party for her, no tearful good-byes, and no telephone calls to stay in touch. Soon after, my 12 year old brother started drinking.

Four years later, I became engaged and invited Anna to my wedding. She wore a beautiful turquoise dress and pearl earrings. For the reception, my father had a cement dance floor built on a small slope in the corner of our backyard overlooking the house. That's where I spent most of the evening, hanging out on the perimeter of that dance floor, a spectator at my own wedding.

I looked out over the sea of people mingling around the swimming pool. On that glorious July evening in 1973, all the buzz was around the televised Watergate hearings, the kidnapping of J. Paul Getty III, and Secretariat's recent Triple Crown win. To the left of the main crowd, I noticed that Anna was standing alone.

While slow dancing with my new husband to *Nights in White Satin*, I looked up to my second bedroom window where Anna nurtured my personal s p a c e. A chest of drawers filled with beautifully pressed cotton clothes always gave me a much-needed sense of order. I can still see her now, putting the iron back in its metal cradle, lighting a non-filtered Chesterfield, and watching television through her tired, yellow-stained eyes.

For the reception, Mother had ordered a gorgeous wildflower arrangement that floated in the middle of the now illuminated swimming pool. The pool was built in the spring of 1968, the same year that Martin Luther King was assassinated. During the riots, I overheard Anna apologizing to my parents for the actions of "her people" when the cities and streets of America turned violent.

Still moving around in small circles to the dreamy lyrics of *Nights* by the Moody Blues, I could see someone from the catering staff washing dishes through the kitchen window. Anna would often take her breaks leaning against the same sink. While she would gaze through the kitchen window into the stillness of the swimming pool, I soaked up her stories like a sponge. Our conversations, standing side by side at that sink, would wax and wane their way through a comfortable blend of sharing and silence. To this day, I can still feel her massive brown arms wrapped around me with my head buried in her chubby, soft bosoms.

Finally, after one of the longest songs in rock history was over, everyone clapped for the bride and groom. As we stepped to one side to have our picture taken, I remembered that buried beneath the dance floor that my father cemented over was the memory of Anna's sweet voice, humming a tune as she hung out our wash.

That night was the last time I saw Anna.

Years later, in an effort to find her, I hired a private investigator.

"I'll need a photograph and her last known address," he informed me over the telephone.

Although he sounded hopeful at the time, it turned out that he would also need her social security number, which I didn't have.

A few years later, I received a call from my sister in California. She was stopped at a traffic light earlier that morning when she received a spiritual "flash" that Anna had died.

"I thought you would like to know," she said. "Something inside...I just knew she was gone."

In a fusion of mixed feelings, I broke down and wept. Clearly my anger and grief was over the loss of Anna, but it was also a reflection of my muddled life during my youth, of never having taken the time to tell her how much she meant to me.

In order to resolve my pain I would have to embrace it. The old me would have allowed the ego to take over by wishing for a different outcome, judging my behavior, or justifying why I didn't tell her. But then I remembered what Jack said, that the soul speaks to us through our feelings, not our minds.

While I can't give back to Anna, I could give forth by sharing with others how much they have inspired me. This helped me to forgive myself, trust that Anna knew how much I loved her, and move on.

Over the years, my mother's story never wavered, leaving me to wonder what made Anna leave without saying good-bye. Today, the truth remains a mystery, dying a slow death in our tidy stack of family secrets.

Sitting in the den, I grab the box of tissue. Salty tears, I once heard, are a sign that there is more to grieve. With my index finger, I brush one from my cheek and take a taste. It is sweet. I close the photo album, the one possession that will go with me in case of a house fire. Then, I get up from the floor, open another box, and continue unpacking.

It occurs to her that she should record this flash of insight in her journal - otherwise she is sure to forget, for she is someone who is always learning and forgetting and obliged to learn again...

– Carol Shields

*Yoga is not about the pose.
It's not the alignment of
toes or hips or shoulders.
It's not about the form.*

*Yoga is an invitation to
explore, not a command
performance. It speaks
the language of the soul.*

*In the flow of breath and
motion, yoga coaxes us
from the confines of the
known, across the silent
threshold into vastness.*

*Yoga is the union of prayer
and movement, guided from
inside. It is healing and the
joy of saying yes to life.*

*Breathe, relax and feel the
body receive its own truth.
The seed of freedom flowers
within each of us whenever
we are open to what's real.*

— Danna Faulds

ANUSARA YOGA

By the end of the sixties, we had burned our bras, marched against the war in Vietnam, and fought for equal rights. We managed to shut down Columbia University, clashed with police at the Democratic National Convention in Chicago and drove President Johnson out of office. For the Woodstock generation, we were a big part of the Movement for a New America, but it wasn't all peace and love.

Although yoga has been around for thousands of years, it was officially introduced to the West in 1969 by Yogi Bhajan. Its philosophy is that within each of us is an enormous reserve of untapped potential, called the Kundalini, which is located in the area towards the base of the spine. By awakening this area, one will feel more vibrant, conscious, and aware.

Beyond that, yoga is hard for me to define - like trying to language air - but in layman's terms it moves internal clutter through the body. Stress, tightness, and tension can be eliminated through deep breathing, stretching, and strengthening. Mentally, I like to think of it as weeding "the garden" of negative, persistent, draining thoughts.

However, my first yoga experience in 1975 would include none of this. The class, held above a health food store, was run by men and women sporting white turbans on their heads with names I couldn't pronounce. Soon after it started, I became dizzy from all the deep breathing. Then my body rebelled against doing the postures because I couldn't get comfortable. When my feet cramped, I went down and landed on my back, unhurt, but decided to stay there until the class was over. I wouldn't take another class for twenty years and, without realizing that not all yoga is created equal, I learned a very important lesson. Find a teacher that resonates with your energy since every class is as different as the person teaching it.

When yoga finally went mainstream in the mid-nineties, I was ready to jump on the bandwagon. Having spotted a flyer taped to the front window of a food co-op, I called the number and shared my yoga experience to a sympathetic woman on the other end of the phone. By the time we finished our conversation, she had given me the confidence to sign up.

She was Iyengar trained, a very detailed, precise practice. While it is very practical for beginners with its emphasis on strict guidelines and correct alignment, there wasn't much s p a c e for something that was a little too reminiscent of my sheltered childhood - self-expression. Still, I managed to stay with it for almost two years.

Then, in 1998, I discovered Anusara, a very heart-centered form of yoga. In fact, Anusara means "flowing with grace" and this uplifting Tantric philosophy of intrinsic Goodness was founded by John Friend in 1997. It was like finding the perfect fitting pair of jeans.

John and I first met at one of his teacher trainings in Baltimore. Upon entering the large, crowded room, he came right over and asked me for my name. Never having met this man whose following now spans the globe, I responded by saying, "Who are you?"

While he greets the last few people who arrive at the workshop, I find a spot in the back of the room and roll out my yoga mat.

It was evident that John Friend knew how to bring out the best in his students. People were drawn to him, not only because he has charisma, but he sees the good in everything and has a divinely tender spirit that exudes joy in what he is doing. He is also committed to honoring and respecting each student's abilities and limitations, and he does it with humor, compassion and knowledge.

Initially, he has us close our eyes and sit with our legs crossed in Sukasana, or easy pose.

"Feel Spirit moving through you in the form of the breath," he starts out in the opening meditation. "The breath moves energy. Feel the breath, feel the stillness between every inhale and exhale. The *s p a c e s* are the gateway to the heart."

Hamming it up with John Friend - before he became famous in the yoga world - at his workshop in Baltimore, Maryland November 3, 1998

His calming demeanor and insightful words balance our energy, thereby allowing us to relax and let go.

Metaphor #1. If my body is tense and my mind active, it will be more difficult to experience conscious awareness and expansion.

"Melt the heart," he says. "The heart is the center for transformation."

Metaphor #2. Melting the heart will increase the odds of me remembering to show compassion not only for myself but for others.

Before we progress into the moving part of the practice, John invites us to set our intention for the workshop.

"In your mind, state your intention clearly and then surrender it."

Without a second thought, I choose *fun* as my intention.

We stretch out our legs and go into a seated forward bend. Silently, I say good morning to my hamstrings, which are extremely tight.

"It doesn't make you a better person if you can get your forehead to your knee," he says, smiling.

His humor will also support my intention to have fun.

"Stay inside with your eyes closed. That way, you won't be tempted to compare yourself to the other people in the room. On the outside, we all look different in the pose, but inside everyone is pushing up against their edge, so just breathe and relax into the stretch."

Metaphor #3. We're many and varied and doing our best in any given moment.

Hearing this supports what I need to hear - that our bodies are all different, that it's okay if I don't look like the person on the cover of *Yoga Journal*, and that it's not so much the pose as what I bring to the pose, an expression of me in that moment and on that day. Tomorrow is another variation of the pose.

Metaphor #4. Keep putting one foot in front of the other and, at the same time, let go of the outcome.

"Seated forward bends are about letting go of resistance and obstacles," he reminds us.

Metaphor #5. Silently, I ask myself what I am resisting in my life.

After we exhale and move out of the forward bend, John asks us to take a moment to feel the changes in the body. I notice a surge of energy running up my legs and it feels utterly sublime. This must be the "yoga buzz" that people talk about.

He invites us to take a few nourishing breaths, allowing time for the energy to circulate through the body.

Metaphor # 6. Allow instead of forcing outcomes.

We gently move up to standing and into Mountain pose, or Tadasana. It is one of the easiest of all the yoga poses, which also makes it one of the most challenging. I have learned that there is more to standing on our two feet than meets the eye.

"Lift and flare the toes and then lay them back down… anchor the four corners of both feet into your mat…hug the muscles in the legs and lift your kneecaps…soften the backs of the knees…lift through the torso and out through the crown of the head…move the shoulders away from the ears and drop the tailbone down. And, remember to melt your heart."

So as not to overwhelm us, John gives us plenty of time to make each subtle adjustment.

"Bring fullness to the pose. Maybe it's about drawing the breath in a little deeper, or being totally present, or lengthening through the spine more."

Metaphor #7. Off the mat, I can choose to give 100% to whatever I'm doing.

From Mountain pose we shift into Uttanasana, or standing forward bend, a pose that is beneficial for settling the mind.

"Let go of the need to get your hands on the floor. Just be content wherever you are in the pose."

Metaphor #8. Trusting that I am exactly where I need to be.

"Now, soften the neck muscles until the crown of the head is facing the earth. In other words, drop the ego."

Metaphor #9. Edging Goodness Out is one acronym for the ego and yoga is the perfect platform to practice disciplining it.

John makes an adjustment on the person next to me while my mind circulates thoughts about lunch. Food is my distraction of choice, a wonder drug that comes with a perfect track record and one that has successfully whisked me away from the present moment since I was two years old.

And then, as if he is reading my mind, John says, "Come back into the body if your mind has wandered."

Metaphor #10. Live in the present moment.

Slowly, we come out of Uttanasana - one vertebrae at a time - into Mountain pose again and stretch from left to right to release the stale air from the side ribs.

"Find the balance between freedom and stability. Can you keep the weight evenly distributed on both feet as you lift through the torso and float the arms from side to side?"

Metaphor #11. This, too, will help me remember to balance structure and flexibility in my daily routine.

John walks around the room, making more adjustments, reminding us to breathe, and keeping us amused. It's easy to have fun in his presence and, with it, my intention remains alive.

He tells us to enjoy the breath, to use the breath to blossom in the pose. The more I breathe into the belly, the more energy I am going to have throughout my day.

Metaphor #12. Practicing yoga has helped me become more aware of the power of the breath and how it reduces stress and anxiety.

Sun Salutations follow, a sequence of postures that begins with Mountain pose and includes Uttanasana, Lunge, Plank, Cobra, and Downward Facing Dog. Each movement is coordinated with the breath, and the flow builds strength and increases flexibility. Sun Salutations are recommended for those days when you don't have time for a full yoga practice. They work every part of the body and are guaranteed to make you feel better.

"Rest if you need to," John interjects between Cobra and Down Dog. "This is your body and only you know it."

Metaphor #13. Honor my limitations.

He decides to wait until after lunch to do inversions, also known as the elixir poses. While they can bring up our fears, they also help us move through them when we're off the mat. Some months back, after I accomplished my first headstand, it was such a thrill that I wanted to call someone on my cell phone and share the good news. And, isn't this what we do in "real" life?

He verified the time with one of his assistants.

"Okay, before we break for lunch, let's do one balancing pose."

I love balancing poses. They are high in value because they require intense focus which allows the mind to rest. They also give us the opportunity to practice loving kindness towards ourselves.

Metaphor #14. If I am feeling shaky in my life, it's better to acknowledge my progress than to berate myself.

John chooses crane pose, a delightful, easy pose that happens to be one of my favorites. We stand on one leg with the other leg lifted, knee bent. Both arms are out in a "t" position with the elbows bent slightly and the hands drooping. I am a starving crane, besotted with thoughts about food.

"Now, find a soft gaze. You are focused on one thing, yet are able to see everyone and everything in the room. This is called drishti," he tells us.

Metaphor #15. My drishti for life is about staying with the task at hand while keeping my eye on the bigger picture.

"Take a risk, go a little wider," John suggests as we go into a standing straddle.

I hear someone wince in pain.

"If you have crossed the line from comfort into struggle, back out of the pose or modify the breath."

Metaphor #16. When my life falls out of the flow, I need to change something.

Everyone is ready for Corpse pose, or Savassana, which is about integrating the practice, keeping the mind still, and allowing myself to surrender so deeply that it feels like the earth is cradling me.

Metaphor #17. I strive to live my life trusting that I will be supported by something greater than myself.

Many consider Savassana to be the most difficult of all poses. This is when I begin to fill up the s p a c e that I have worked so hard to clear, often with my "to do" list. So, once again, I practice releasing my thoughts by bringing my awareness back to the breath and my intention.

"You're no longer working the breathe, you're watching it," I hear him say.

After a morning of yoga, I have returned to my natural state of being, an empty vessel once again. We move out of Savassana and come full circle into Sukasana where John invites us to chant the sound "OM" three times.

"'Om' symbolizes that we are all connected to the same Source," he says.

John is right. The vibration from the primal sound from which all things are created fills my body and I feel at one with the Universe again. I have decided that yoga will only change my life for the better.

Kater doing her 'OM' thing in Warrior II Pose at the fort in Old San Juan, Puerto Rico.
March 2, 2005

*Thirty-two years after my first yoga experience, I attended a series of Kundalini classes and found that they motivated me to take deeper risks, go beyond what I thought was possible, trust myself and connect to my inner strength.

The way we do anything is the way we do everything.

– unknown

Everything in moderation, including moderation.

— from the teachings of Buddha

BALANCE

1974 ushered in a new chapter for me. In June of that year, I moved from a one bedrooom apartment to live off the land in Colorado. It was a spiritual journey of sorts, one that would take me from "affluenza" to deprivation to discovering the gratifying *s p a c e* between the two.

Three months before, in March, my husband and I interviewed for a job to work on a dude ranch just outside of Gunnison in southwest Colorado. At the time, it sounded perfect. We would live in a cabin by the river, work five days a week, and take weekends off to explore the surrounding area.

In preparation to leave Ann Arbor, we agreed to take only those possessions that would fit into our fuel efficient, bronze Vega. The rest, we decided, could be stashed in a friend's garage.

"If we stay in Colorado," I said to Alan, "we'll just have to come back for our stuff."

So, with our two basset hounds, Herbert and Beatrice, we got on Interstate 94 and headed west.

Two years before, Alan and I met at my cousin's wedding in Cleveland. He was 6'3" tall next to my 5'4" height, and head-turning handsome. There was something about his eyes that drew me in - mysterious and wise and intelligent - with eyebrows that were lushly thick and dark, hair that fell below his ears, and a mustache.

He had numerous interests, but his real passion was photography. At my cousin's wedding, when he approached me with a Hasselblad strapped over his shoulder, I couldn't resist his offer to photograph me by the shores of Lake Erie.

In spending what little time we had together that weekend, I learned that he grew up in a very liberal, New England family. His parents, including two sisters, lived a similar lifestyle to mine, but their values were different. They nurtured the passions of their children, encouraged free thinking, and supported their decision to attend progressive schools.

I grew up in a more conservative, protected environment where appearances, status, and things were valued. My father, a successful insurance executive, worked hard to keep his family comfortably grounded in an upper middle-class lifestyle. We had a nice home in the suburbs, horseback riding lessons, and revolving credit to maintain the growing trend of over-consumption in the postwar era of the 1950s.

Like most of my friends, I was a shopper who loved to scout the pages of *Seventeen* for the latest styles. I bought patterned stockings and vinyl boots. I wore bellbottom pants and accessorized my face with Twiggy eyelashes and white lipstick. All of this was integrated into my wardrobe of Pappagallo shoes, Villager sweaters, and pocketbooks with removable covers to match my outfits.

For the sole purpose of accommodating the growing collection of clothes for his wife and three daughters, Dad built floor-to-ceiling closets that were a foot deep and covered the entire length of an upstairs hallway. Walls were turned into shelves, drawers were crafted on the sides of built-in beds, and dead *s p a c e* was turned into cubbies for accessories.

Three years after graduating from high school, in the summer of 1972, I met Alan. After my cousin's wedding, our Massachusetts-to-Maryland courtship took flight. At the time, he was taking a year off from the University of Michigan. During our biweekly visits, he introduced me to various kinds of music, controversial authors, and radical ideas. I loved to listen to his stories about Big Ten football games, fraternity parties, and campus life. In one conversation, he casually mentioned that The Doors played at his freshman dance in 1967.

Eleven months after we met, on July 7, 1973, we were married. That fall, we moved to Ann Arbor where he was going to finish out his last year of architecture school. Like Berkeley, student unrest had been a big part of campus life at Michigan in the 1960s. Women's Liberation, the Black Power movement, and affirmative action all had strong reverberations there.

While Alan went to school during the day, I worked for a real estate company, muscling my way through to pay the bills in a boring 9-to-5 job. Off the clock, however, Ann Arbor was stimulating - watching a naked student cart-wheel across The Diag, the ever present Hare Krishnas standing on the street corners, and the woman in her eighties riding her bicycle with pastel butterflies painted on her cheeks. At home, we hung out with his college buddies, lived on a diet of pizza, and raised two puppies. But even Ann Arbor, with her ability to expand my horizons and nourish my rebellious spirit, wouldn't be able to tame my restless soul.

So, on the first day of June in 1974, in our two-door Chevrolet Vega hatchback, we left for Colorado. I remember that Patty Hearst's kidnapping dominated the news over the radio, gasoline was a whopping 55 cents a gallon, and the trip cost us just under one hundred dollars to reach the dude ranch in Gunnison.

When we arrived four days later, we found the 1,000 acre ranch beautifully situated in a narrow valley. The main house, or "big house" as the caretaker called it, was built in the center of the ranch with guest cabins scattered around it. Our cabin was at the far end of the property, away from the big house of course.

Alan and I loved Colorado with its surreal landscapes, clean air, and low-key attitude. But the job proved disappointing. The cabin by the river was nice, but it didn't make up for the back

*This photograph of me was taken shortly after
Alan and I celebrated our
elaborate backyard wedding in 1973.
As a joke, I made postcards out of the picture
and sent them to family and friends.
On the back, I wrote: Marriage is . . . .*

This picture of Alan was taken in Ann Arbor, Michigan.
1973

breaking work and long days cleaning guest cabins, mending fences, and tilling soil for the owner's vegetable garden. In one month, we only had two days off which, as salaried employees, was not only draining us physically but mentally and spiritually as well.

Just under a month after our arrival, we left the ranch with no idea where we were going or what we would do for money. We aimlessly drove around for a couple of days and ended up in Telluride. The following day, I called home "collect."

Mother answered the phone. After listening to our plight, she said, "You know, Caroline is living in Montrose with her husband."

I felt a fist-size knot in my stomach. Growing up, Caroline lived on the same street and, even though her parents and my parents were great friends, she and I never connected. The fact that she was a couple of years older than I did nothing to bridge the gap.

Then there was the transportation issue. While I stood on the corner for the bus, Caroline was driven to school by the family chauffeur, whom they called "Sleepy." Of course, whatever she wore I didn't have and wherever she partied I wasn't invited. But, the worst part was that I actually believed that whomever she dated wouldn't even notice me.

Naturally, this mismatch of two souls had nothing to do with her and everything to do with my low self-esteem at the time. I told myself there was no way that she would want me as a friend, nor could I possibly measure up to what I thought her standards were at the time.

"She doesn't have a phone in Montrose, only an address," Mother told me.

"I'll take it," I said, waving to Alan for a piece of paper while he was getting stoned in the passenger seat of the car.

While I was waiting for him to find something to write on, Mother told me that she and my father had attended Caroline and Jay's wedding. Before they were married, Jay had a beautiful ash blonde ponytail down to his waist. For the wedding, he cut off that ponytail and Caroline wore it pinned to the side of her hair.

"Would you believe it was an exact color match?" Mother said. "And, you never saw a more handsome couple than those two."

Alan finally approached the car with a piece of paper and pen so that I could scribble down Caroline's address.

"You know, she's pregnant," Mother warned me.

I hung up the phone and decided to banish my past with Caroline and start anew. It was time to clean the slate. Besides, we were desperate. So, with our plan hatched, we left Telluride for Montrose, arriving the next day to find an old iron cattle gate that led to the house where she and Jay lived.

We were relieved to see Caroline was home when we pulled up. She looked fabulous and vibrant and surprisingly glad to see us. Our thought was to spend a few days there. Instead, we stayed for five months.

The old rental cabin where she and Jay lived had no heat, electricity, phone, or hot water. A two-seater outhouse stood near the vegetable garden with an empty, run-down barn a few hundred yards away.

Inside, the kitchen shelves were exposed yet mesmerizing to look at. Lined with beautiful glass jars in various shapes and sizes, they were filled with an array of non-perishable foods in assorted earthy colors - beans, peas, whole grain flours, brown rice, herbs, spices, and dried fruit. A hand pump in the sink provided drinking water.

As a teenager growing up in the sixties, I remembered reading stories about the so-called simple life. Every Friday after school, I would bury myself in my mother's wing chair and pour through the new issue of *Life* magazine. There, in my parents' living room, images of campus unrest, hippies in San Francisco, and living off the land would come alive for me.

Now, Caroline's lifestyle gave me the opportunity to experience what I had missed out on. She introduced me to vegetarian cooking, juicing, and drying herbs. Together, we made homemade whole wheat bread. I also helped her haul water in buckets, wash clothes, and pull weeds from the vegetable garden.

To pay for gas, rent, and provisions, we pooled our money, doing odd jobs baling hay, working construction, and waiting tables. There were weekly ten mile trips into Montrose to take showers, make phone calls, and shop the local thrift stores for clothes. On the way home, we picked up fresh goat's milk and eggs from a local rancher.

A little over a month after we arrived in Montrose, and weeks of pleading with the nation "to put Watergate behind us," Richard Nixon gave his resignation speech. Since there was no television, we piled into Jay's truck and drove 30 miles to a friend's house. It was the night before my Dad's 49th birthday, August 8, 1974.

I thought about my father and wondered if he was thinking about me in Colorado, wearing war torn jeans, eating meals from the garden, and hanging out with women who wore studs in their noses, unusual in 1974. Looking back, one of his biggest fears was that I would become a hippy, leave home, and drop out. And, since we attract our fears, that's exactly what happened.

Now, as President Nixon was making his transition, I was beginning to wonder about my life, too. Living a simple life in Colorado seemed like a good place to embrace what I thought would support that, but it was beginning to feel more like deprivation and hardship.

As the days in Montrose turned into weeks, tempers began to flare as jobs grew scarce. The weather turned cold early that year and money was running out. Our Chevrolet Vega was repossessed. By early October, Caroline, now eight months pregnant, moved back to Baltimore.

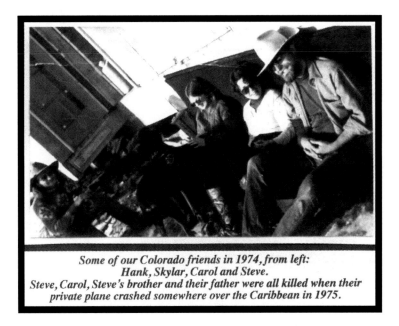

Some of our Colorado friends in 1974, from left:
Hank, Skylar, Carol and Steve.
Steve, Carol, Steve's brother and their father were all killed when their
private plane crashed somewhere over the Caribbean in 1975.

Six weeks later, Jay, Alan, and I, along with our combined pack of five dogs, drove straight through from Montrose to Maryland. The reality that we were broke, humiliated, and scared made the long trip even more tedious and unbearable. Two days later, exhausted, he dropped us off at the bottom of my parents' driveway.

After living with my parents for a month, Alan and I rented an affordable apartment on the other side of town. We pooled our stuff from various places around the country - our friend's garage in Ann Arbor, Alan's parents' house where they had since moved to in upstate New York, and my parents' basement in Maryland.

Since many of our possessions and wedding gifts no longer aligned with our taste and lifestyle, we kept only those things that were beautiful, useful, wanted, and that we loved and would enjoy. The rest would be sold or given away. It was a process that required desire, focus, and patience, but eventually we began to feel a sense of material balance in our lives. We also realized that the more we simplified, the less we wanted.

Four years after we left Colorado for Maryland, Alan and I amicably went our separate ways. I rented a charming, one-room walkup and stayed there for ten years. With limited storage *s p a c e,* I was force to implement the "one in, one out" guideline when buying things. Then, three years later, I bought a one bedroom co-op and scaled back another layer.

After Jay dropped us off at my parents' house in November of 1974, I never saw him again. Years later, I ran into Caroline at her mother's funeral. After the service, we laughed about the contrast of our charmed lives growing up and living off the land in Colorado.

I shared with her that we never know who is going to inspire us, that it can be the person we least expect. Caroline was a humble example of someone "I had nothing in common with," yet she changed the course of my life forever. Through her, I was able to experience the sweet balance between excess and scarcity.

Sheer poverty never made anyone more peaceful; extreme but voluntary austerity is often the flip side of extravagance. The mark of successful detachment from possessions is not how few of them we have around us, but how little s p a c e they occupy in our minds.

– Maggie Kramm

You must learn to welcome consciously the most unexpected events of life, to be entirely transparent in front of them, without any motive, either right or wrong. At that moment, avoid all judgment, for you do not know what law is in operation.

— Lizelle Reymond

DEBEN

Once I made the decision to stop drinking, it was like raising the blinds on a window after twenty years. On February 25, 1987, I stepped out and crossed the threshold from darkness to light. It was during this early stage of my long climb back that an African American healer finally got me out of my head and into my heart.

I first heard about Deben from my friend, Ted. Years before, Ted and I crossed paths through business. Then we didn't see each other for a while until, one Sunday morning, I ran into him at an A.A. meeting.

After the meeting, we went to brunch and Deben's name came up. Ted told me that he conducted workshops, mostly in his home, where he attracted people who were willing to venture out beyond their comfort zone.

"You have to experience this guy," Ted told me over Eggs Benedict.

He paused to ask the waitress to bring him some more skim milk for his coffee.

"For one thing," Ted said, "he uses no last name. He even refused to give in to the local bank when he opened an account with them."

I put my fork down.

"He also drinks wheat grass juice and spirilina."

Now, at the time, I had never heard of wheat grass juice or spirilina.

"Deben is amazing. This is a guy who can sail through the night without sleep and still look refreshed when the sun comes up. I have no idea how he does it."

Having always been drawn to people who think outside of the box, I asked Ted to let me know when Deben was offering his next workshop. I was ready to take on a personal challenge. After being sober for six months, I realized that giving up alcohol was relatively easy. Coming face to face with the reason that I drank would be another matter.

We split the check and walked out.

Sure enough, a couple of months later, Ted called to tell me about Deben's upcoming workshop.

Without hesitation, I said, "I'm there."

Two weeks later, on a Friday afternoon, my bag was packed when Ted picked me up in his tan Chevy wagon. In a matter of minutes, we were on our way to Deben's house in Washington, D.C.

From my co-op in Baltimore, it took us about an hour. As we gathered miles toward our destination, I could feel the stress in my body melt away like a pile of soft snow in the mid-afternoon sun. In what seemed like no time at all, we were turning off of a busy road onto Deben's tree-lined street.

The house, probably built around the turn of the nineteenth century, was sizable with a big porch, cathedral ceilings and stained glass windows. It was located in what was once a fashionable area in Washington. Now, the neighborhood looked a little long in the tooth. I noticed that the door was ajar as we approached the front steps.

Veet Karm, Deben's housemate, greeted us in the foyer. The scene was casual– "shoes off, be comfortable, hang out until we're ready" kind of casual. We dropped our bags by the door and split up. Ted wandered into the kitchen while I went upstairs to use the bathroom. When I came back down, my friend Lucie was standing in the hallway, a portrait of calm surrender. She and I gathered in the living room, where we passed time catching up.

DEBEN
"The Enlightened One"

After what seemed like an inordinate amount of time, Deben finally breezed in the room, rang out a quick "hello," introduced himself, and promptly left to answer the telephone. He was rail thin with short cropped hair and, surprisingly, very ordinary looking.

I watched him flit from room to room like a hummingbird while the rest of the workshop participants straggled in with their backpacks and duffel bags. The scent of emotional neediness was in the air. Other than Deben's friendly one-liners, everyone else kept pretty much to themselves.

By 7:30 p.m. or so (remember, casual), everyone had arrived. Shortly thereafter, Deben announced that he was ready to start the workshop.

"I'll meet you downstairs in the basement," he said, "and bring all of your belongings with you."

So, like good little soldiers, everyone padded down the stairs in silence.

The basement was definitely a statement in function over fashion. It was one big room with pine paneling and wall-to-wall shag carpeting. Two old sofas were arranged in an "L" shape against one corner wall and in the opposite corner was a temperature controlled saltwater tank, big enough for two people to float in. To the left of the tank was a bed sheet hanging from the ceiling to shelter a combined laundry room, toilet, and sink.

I plopped down against the wall near the saltwater tank, closed my eyes, and allowed my mind to meander. Two years before, I had flown to Israel to visit my friend Jason who was going to medical school in Tel Aviv. Our plan was to go to Jerusalem, head south to Eliat, and then drive to the northern part of the country. In between those two destinations, we spent a day at The Dead Sea.

Located 1,310 feet below sea level, The Dead Sea is the lowest elevation on Earth. From all over the world, people come for the healing properties found in the mineral rich mud and salt water. What makes it extraordinary is the contrast - hauntingly still, yet alluring.

As soon as Jason and I arrived there, we covered ourselves in mud that was stored in large barrels. Then we stepped into the tepid water where, for hours, we floated like buoys. As I laid effortlessly on my back with ankles crossed and hands clasped behind my head, a luxurious sense of inner peace washed over me. For the first time in my life, I felt "at one" with everything.

I took this picture of Jason (on left) floating in The Dead Sea with his two roommates, 1986. All three were studying medicine at the University of Tel Aviv in Israel.

Now, I was contemplating Deben's saltwater tank as a sign that this weekend might be another spiritual experience for me. After opening my eyes, I noticed that everyone had staked out their sleeping *s p a c e* and settled in. The first two people down the stairs had already grabbed the sofas. Now, the only place left was my cozy little spot between the stairs and the saltwater tank.

How perfect, I thought.

When the rustling in the room simmered down, Deben appeared and asked us to gather in a circle. With his bare feet and spirilina drink in tow, he opened with a single guideline.

"Who we see here and what we say here stays here. This allows us to feel safe in order to speak openly and honestly."

This was serious business, but Deben's timing, tone of voice, and facial expressions cracked me up. Oddly, I was the only one who thought it was funny. Paying no attention to my lone outburst, he asked if we had any questions about anonymity.

I held my breath, knowing from experience that there always seems to be one person who needs clarification. It's not a big deal except that, invariably, one question turns into another one and, before we know it, half an hour has passed. This could threaten my sleep schedule.

To my surprise and delight, no one had any questions.

Deben then asked each of us to introduce ourselves and share with the group why we were there. What sounded like eight different stories were really the same. We all wanted something. We may not have known what it was, but we were looking just the same.

After the last person shared, Deben had us close our eyes for a short meditation. So far, he appeared to be a collage of charisma, love, and authenticity.

I glanced at the wristwatch on the woman sitting next to me. Already, a little over an hour had passed and, according to my plan, all was going well.

As we were coming out of the meditation and back into the room, Deben said to the group, "Tell me who you are."

No one said anything.

I guess we needed more time to transition out of the meditation because there we sat, staring at each other.

"Tell me who you are," he repeated.

We all looked around the circle to see who would start. Not being able to stand the silence, I decided to jump in and get it over with.

"Well," I quipped, "I am a recovering alcoholic and I have my own catering business. I also live alone."

Done. That seemed easy enough.

When no one spoke, Deben stated again, "Tell me who you are."

Everyone then looked at the person sitting to my left as if to assume that, instead of randomly volunteering, we might as well just go around the circle.

So, the woman sitting next to me reluctantly spoke up. She was a free spirit type with long, flowing brown hair wearing one of those awful looking tent dresses to hide her ballooning weight. I guessed that she was in her early fifties.

"Well, I am a massage therapist, a grieving massage therapist. My mother died two months ago."

Again, there was silence.

I could see Deben from the corner of my eye sipping his green drink and slowly pacing around the room.

"Next person." he said. "Tell me who you are."

It was Ted's turn, my friend, the guy who brought me here.

"I am the father of three beautiful girls and in the process of getting a divorce."

Ted released a resounding breath and smiled proud.

Making no eye contact with anyone in particular, Deben said, "Keep going. Tell me who you are."

The person seated in Lotus on Ted's right shared that he worked at a natural foods store. He had medium-length chestnut hair pulled back in a thick ponytail, wire rim glasses, and skin that looked like a bar of Dove soap.

Flashing a gap-toothed smile, he told us that he liked to play the banjo, hike and watch foreign flicks.

I looked around the circle. We were halfway there - four down, four more to go.

"Next." Deben said, "Tell me who you are."

A woman, probably in her mid sixties, told the group that she was an O.R. nurse and a published author.

"I wrote a book on shade gardening. My husband left me after 30 years of marriage when I fell in love with a woman," she confessed.

"Next."

Lucie opened with a shy laugh and looked down at the floor, sighing, "Well, I am in social worker. My boyfriend has been sick for almost a year now and a lot of my time and energy has been focused on taking care of him. Right now, I don't know who I am."

I never liked her boyfriend, probably because he was a chauvinist and would never be able to respect, honor, and appreciate women without feeling threatened by them. I could never figure out what Lucie saw in him, though I had no trouble figuring out what he saw in her.

Deben waited for several seconds before breaking the silence.

"Next."

"Besides being a waitress, I don't have much to say," a young woman in her twenties said. She seemed agitated, like someone had talked her into coming to the workshop. Otherwise, she was attractive in a wholesome sort of way, that is if you didn't look at the phallic looking tattoos running down her willowy legs.

Deben seemed unaffected by her angry undertone.

"Next."

The last to go was a yuppie type in her late thirties. She told us that she was married to a wonderful man who was supportive and faithful, but boring.

"We have two small children," she said, "and everything in my life appears to be fine, but I'm not happy. Something is missing."

I decided on the spot what her problem was. The passion had been siphoned out of her marriage due to the daunting task of raising kids.

Finally, all eight of us told Deben who we were. There was a caterer, a massage therapist, a divorced salesman, an employee at a natural foods store, a nurse and published author, a social worker, an angry waitress and an unhappy yuppie mom. It was a good mix of people, and the ratio of women to men was normal for this kind of workshop - six to two.

Then I heard it again.

"Tell me who you are."

Although everyone had taken a turn, I was thinking that Deben wanted more information in order to get to know us better. So, once again, I took the lead. I told the group that I exercised and ate well. I was born with an organization gene. I read a lot because I hadn't owned a television for six years.

Then I held my breath, waiting for Deben to give me some indication that I was on the right track.

"Next."

Like Pavlov's dog, I released the air from my lungs. Apparently, "next" meant that whatever was said wasn't what Deben wanted to hear.

Then the massage therapist to my left spoke, explaining that she was a widow and collected antique jewelry. Again, she reminded us that her mother had died but added that her son hadn't spoken to her in two years.

At the time, the A.C.O.A. movement (Adult Children of Alcoholics) was in its prime. Children choosing to avoid contact with their parents in order to heal was nothing out of the ordinary.

Even before we entered the basement, I noticed that this woman carried herself like the weight of the world was on her shoulders, and she had the body to prove it under that tent dress.

"Next."

Ted shared that he was also a recovering alcoholic with five years sobriety, an only child, and a hopeless Buckeye fan. We were rivals, my having been married to a Wolverines fan.

When it was time for the natural foods guy to share, he hesitated for a minute, like he might cry. He told us that his girlfriend had broken up with him a couple of months ago.

"We were together for almost three years. I want to honor her decision, but I am really bummed out about it. That's why I decided to come to this workshop, to get some insight on what part I played in the breakup."

Now, there's my kind of man - mature, respectful, and responsible. He was so in touch with his feminine side that I might have actually considered asking him out except for one slight problem. High on my list of criteria is that the person be able to remember where they were when President Kennedy was assassinated. This guy, in 1963, wasn't even a fleeting thought in his parents' eyes.

Next in line was the woman, the nurse and author, whose husband left her.

"Right now, I am going through a mid-life crisis. My job at the hospital is incredibly stressful. And, now my two daughters can't deal with the fact that I am romantically involved with a woman."

Without giving Deben the opportunity to ask us who we were, Lucie with the creepy boyfriend jumped in. She and I had a lot in common - eating sushi, meditating by candlelight, and going to Al-Anon meetings. Her energy was light and spirited, and I was beginning to sense we were going to need every bit of it by the end of the evening.

Lucie shared that she was one of four kids, the oldest daughter who had to take care of her siblings while her single mother worked the nightshift at a local brewery plant.

"Early on, I learned how to be a caretaker. That's who I am, a caretaker. I'm very good at it, but it's no longer serving me."

Sitting there listening to her, the lines appeared to be blurred. I didn't know if her suffering stemmed from taking care of others or living with her boyfriend who was a toad.

Next in line was the angry waitress with the tattoos on her legs. This time, however, she offered more information.

"I am a single mother with a two year old. As soon as he goes to school, I want to get a degree in psychology. Eventually, I want to work with kids."

I tapped my neighbor on the shoulder and pointed a finger to my wrist. She looked at her watch and whispered, "10:20."

Then the yuppie married to the boring man with two children offered her second installment of who she was.

"When I was 15," she told us, "both of my parents were killed in a freak car accident. After that, I went to live with my maternal grandparents until it was time to go to college. After graduating, I managed a high-end retail store with twenty employees."

Twiddling my fingers, I was grateful for my life with all of its flaws and broken dreams and loss. I once heard a teacher say that if everyone threw their problems in a circle, most likely each person would gladly take back their own.

We went on to finish the second round and then a third. By the time the fourth round was over, my body was telling me that it was time for bed.

Deben pressed on, filling the stale, heavy air with his "mantra du jour."

"Tell me who you are."

Ready to say something really profound, I took a deep breath in and shared that I know everything happens for my highest good and I create my own reality.

There. Whether or not I believed it, this might be enough for Deben to wrap things up for the evening.

All was quiet.

As soon as I heard him say tell me who you are, I got up and supported my back against the wall.

And so it went, a circle of seekers mumbling in monotones. I started to borrow other people's careers, childhood traumas, hobbies, favorite foods, and success stories. Then they started using mine. We were repeating ourselves and, toward the end, making things up.

As the night droned on, so did we.

Clearly, everyone was waiting for Deben to say something - anything - except those dreaded five words. Something like, "Excellent, now that's what I'm looking for!" By 3:00 a.m., the correct response still hadn't surfaced.

I got up to go to the bathroom for the umpteenth time. In Deben's workshops, there were no formal breaks. If you had to go, then you just quietly left the circle.

After returning to the group, I laid on the floor and wondered why we couldn't continue the workshop tomorrow. At first, I was angry at Ted for getting me into this. Then, I turned it inward, berating myself for having paid someone to keep me up all night. Even as a kid, I hated going to those sleepless slumber parties.

Now, to keep from falling asleep in Deben's basement, I stood up and walked around, half-dazed. Maybe if I sighed loud enough, Deben would let us go to sleep. He picked up on my energy, or lack of it.

"Notice what is going on inside of you right now," Deben said. "Being tired is a sign that you are resisting something. What is it that you are resisting right now?"

"Who cares," I mumbled under my breath.

I remembered a woman who approached me after I chaired an A.A. meeting, telling me that if God is putting me through the wringer, then I must be worth laundering.

"Next." Deben said with his hands clasped behind his back, "Tell me who you are."

The process continued for another couple of hours until around 5:00 a.m.. . .and then it happened. The dark side of sleep deprivation finally blew and all hell broke loose.

I got up off of the floor and, like a frustrated two year old, started screaming and yelling. I told Deben I didn't know who I was, nor for that matter did I care. I told him that I didn't want to play this stupid game anymore and that he could keep his money. All I wanted to do was go to sleep and be left alone.

After my tantrum turned into a dismal swamp of tears, I crumbled into a heap on the floor and wept, not even caring that I had lost all control in front of the group.

The silence in the room was absolute.

Growing up, I was punished for showing emotion, especially if it wasn't expressed in a ladylike fashion. Now, in Deben's workshop, too exhausted to care, I laid on the floor, a puddle of grief, until every tear drained from my body.

Someone shoved a box of Kleenex across the floor, but I wasn't ready to "erase" what I had been through to bring an end to the madness. The last "tell me who you are" had finally been put to rest.

I opened my eyes and scanned the room. I noticed the widow with the dead mother and the estranged son fidgeting with the hem on her balloon-shaped tent dress. The angry waitress was sitting against the wall with her eyes staring at the ceiling. Ted looked at me as if to say *I owe you big time.*

Deben invited us to form a circle. Once we settled in, he filled the last remaining *s p a c e*, and rested his eyes on the shag carpet. Then, before speaking, he made contact with each one of us.

"In this very moment," he said, "you have just witnessed who she is."

What? I thought.

"Now, close your eyes."

He paused to give us a few moments to absorb what we had just witnessed.

"Who we are is not about what we do," Deben informed us, "and, who you are is not about your job."

I finally blew my nose.

"Who you are is not about the way your body looks, the clothes that you wear, the amount of money that you have in your bank account, or how many possessions you own."

I felt my heart gradually returning to a normal rhythm.

"We say who we think we are out of our need to be accepted, or to be nice. So, we tell others what we want them to hear without ever investigating who we really are. Basically, we go through life faking it."

I repositioned myself in order to avoid getting a cramp in my right leg.

"Other people, including society, think they have a handle on you. The truth is that no one has a handle on you."

I looked over at Ted, who was moving his head from side to side. As he stretched out his legs, I realized that all of my life I found myself in the company of people who didn't really want to know who I was. Instead, they wanted to mold me into someone that I wasn't.

Deben was a man of few words which also gave him the ability to attract people's attention when he spoke.

He went on. "Who we are is a summation of our life as we live day to day. Our living is in the culmination of all that we have learned about ourselves - the wisdom that we collect, the people that we meet, the things that we do."

Deben repositioned himself from lotus to sukassana.

"Who you were last year doesn't exist. Right now, you are not the same person that you were yesterday because of the experiences that you brought with you today. Therefore, there is no end to knowing who you are…and that is what creates the mystery and the excitement in life."

I couldn't get comfortable, so I grabbed a couple of pillows and propped myself up against the wall again. Not surprisingly, I wasn't tired anymore.

"We are always discovering new things about ourselves, and when the changes unfold, you will see a different side of yourself."

Deben looked over at me and said, "Your feelings opened the door to self-awareness."

I glanced around the circle. When my eyes locked with Ted's, he winked.

"We want to avoid our feelings by staying in our head," Deben said. "We want to justify, analyze, blame, and try to figure things out. Now, there's nothing wrong with that, but it's not the same as feeling them. Remember, feelings don't lie."

At the workshop, I had been in my head the whole time to avoid anger, sadness, and frustration.

Deben closed his eyes.

"The longest journey in your life is the 12 inches from your head to your heart."

Then he took in a long, slow, deep breath and released it. "The art of healing is based on self-knowledge and therein, lies our power."

Ted sneezed abruptly, startling the mature guy with the skin like a bar of Dove whose girlfriend broke up with him. It was my turn to slide the box of Kleenex across the rug.

"Spiritually speaking, the bottom line is that if you were to ever figure out who you are then, in that very moment, you can choose to either live or die."

With that, he picked up his empty bottle of spirilina and made his way to the stairs.

That statement went right over my head. Maybe he was reaffirming that we never really know who we are.

Then he turned in our direction and said, "Now, get some rest."

Everyone stared into the air.

Finally, I got up to go to the bathroom and brushed my teeth while the rest of the group got ready for bed. Then I opened my sleeping bag and crawled in. With my eyes opened, I thought about Deben and how he created a safe environment for me to express my feelings without trying to judge, shame, or control me.

I also wondered why it never occurred to me - in the *s p a c e* of nine hours - to say that I didn't know who I was. I muffled a spontaneous laugh and gave myself a big hug. I felt at peace with myself, just like that day floating in The Dead Sea.

Surrounded by goose down, I rolled onto my right side. That night, I finally got it that who I am is not tangible. For years, I had identified myself by where I lived, what I did, whom I hung out with, and how I dressed. Now, who I am is as simple as just being myself in the present moment, for it is always changing anyway.

Then, with a renewed heart, everything went still around me...

I had no idea what time it was when Deben sounded the wake-up bell. As I stretched out my arms and legs, I remembered him saying there is no time in the spiritual world. I smiled and made a mental note to put that on my list of new concepts. Then I got up and prepared myself for the second day.

After that weekend, I continued to attend his workshops. Once, I went to see him for an individual session. Another time, Terry and I went together. At one workshop, he walked around banging pots and pans while we meditated, saying, "Let nothing disturb you!"

In the spirit of sobriety, I had to drain the emotional, mental, and spiritual clutter in order to make *s p a c e* for the light to fill my life again. Deben's ability to push me beyond my limits allowed me to remember a side of myself that I had long ago forgotten. And he did it by just being who he was, whatever that was, in any given moment throughout that landmark weekend.

Some people come into our lives and quickly go.
Some stay for a while, leave footprints on our hearts,
and we are never, ever the same.

— Flavia

Unlike your genetics, you have a choice
over what foods you eat and their
subsequent impact on your well-being.

– Mitch Thrower

DETOX YOUR KITCHEN

Back in the seventies, when I decided to clean up my personal *s p a c e*, I started in the kitchen. Although I prefer to maintain a home that is functional, clutter-free, and clean, it is my kitchen - and especially my refrigerator - that I consider sacred ground. If I want to nourish my body in a way that supports a healthy lifestyle, then a refrigerator that is cluttered, dirty, and filled with old, moldy food isn't going to align with my intention. Call it compulsive, but I even put my sponge in the dishwasher every night and wash my tea towels and potholders often.

Throughout my ten year career as a caterer, and now as a professional organizer and home stager, I have discovered that many people have no idea what is in their pantry, refrigerator, or freezer. Many refrigerators look like food junkyards, so packed with stuff that even finding *s p a c e* for anything is impossible. Some labels on spices and processed foods date back to the Nixon administration. One client had so many cans of tomato products - paste, sliced, sauce, diced, and whole - that she had to store them in her basement to make room for the tomato goods that her husband continued to bring home. I say all of this without judgment because I have my own set of issues.

One of them is sugar, and while I consumed my share of it growing up, my mother fed us well. Rarely did she give in to Wonder Bread, canned soup, or T.V. dinners. She bought Pepperidge Farm bread, made delectable soups with stock made of beef and chicken bones, and served fresh flounder for Sunday brunch. In those days, most people ate frozen fish and usually only on Friday.

Not surprisingly, infants have to acquire a taste for sweets and overly salty, processed foods. Therefore, retraining our taste buds from processed junk to whole foods is a gradual one. In time, you will notice that the more whole foods you consume, the better they are going to make you feel. Their abundance of vitamins, minerals, flavor, and fiber are not only highly beneficial and nourishing, but they will increase your energy levels and leave you feeling more satisfied.

When grocery shopping, spend the majority of your money in the perimeters of the store. This is where you will find the best value for your overall health - "live" fresh produce, organic meat, chicken, seafood, whole grain breads, and dairy products.

Most processed foods, i.e. canned, frozen, or prepackaged, are located in the interior aisles. Nowadays, there are enough brands made with organic ingredients and healthy oils to justify buying them. Also, the money you save by eating at home will allow you to buy organic. If something isn't organic, choose brands with "natural" ingredients. Unhealthy food is another form of clutter that will compromise your health.

1. Pitch the food clutter from your refrigerator and freezer, i.e., anything that is moldy, rancid, and old. Toss old condiments, especially the ones that haven't been used in a long time. After cleaning your fridge with soap and water, begin to restock it with healthier food.

2. Empty out your pantry completely. That way, you can see what you have, what needs to go, and what you will want to keep. If something has chemical additives, artificial preservatives, hydrogenated oils, harmful sweeteners, or anything else that you can't pronounce, throw it out. If you are truly serious about changing your eating habits, toss the white stuff, too - flour, sugar, and rice. If you must keep it on hand, buy organic. Then clean the shelves and restock your pantry with healthier canned and processed foods.

3. Weed out your herbs and spices. If the basil, tarragon, oregano, and rosemary are army green in color, then it is bitter and will ruin the taste of anything that you put them in. Your body is not a garbage disposal, so if something smells rancid, throw it out. Store dried herbs, spices, whole grain flours, nuts, and seeds in the refrigerator.

4. Empty every cabinet and drawer. Toss containers that don't have matching lids. If you end up with 30 sets, give away 15. Discard chipped glasses, cracked bowls and plates, broken gadgets, utensils that are hard to use, and anything else that you haven't used for the last five years. Decluttering will also give you more counter s p a c e, something we never seem to have enough of.

5. Clean out your recipe box, keeping only those that you want and that align with how you want to eat _now_. Unless you have time to test them, toss out the piles of magazine and newspaper recipes that you have saved over the years. Recycle any cookbooks that you don't use. Invest in one "reference type" cookbook, such as _The Joy of Cooking_, that provides information on almost everything including preparation tips, seasoning ideas, and cooking times.

6. Since lasting change is a process, start by preparing one whole food meal a week, then one a day. Use the 80/20 rule, meaning that 80% of your daily food intake is healthy. Strive to eat "the colors of the rainbow", i.e., consume as many different colors at one meal as possible. One example of a colorful, whole food meal would be broiled flounder or chicken, baked sweet potatoes, and a medley of steamed fresh vegetables.

7. To simplify, choose meals with similar cooking times that allow you to do two things at once. A whole chicken can share the oven with a pan of potatoes, scrubbed clean with their skins left on (both take about an hour). While they are cooking, make a salad to go with it. Or, cook a salmon filet while a pot of quinoa is simmering on the stove (both take 20-25 minutes).

Round it out with some sliced tomatoes and a sautéed or steamed green vegetable.

8. Whole food snacks can be as easy as fresh fruit and cheese, a handful of organic nuts, a hard boiled egg, cooked edamame beans, or a lightly toasted rice cake topped with peanut butter, hummus, or mashed beans.

9. Reduce stress. If you are avoiding certain foods, then don't keep them in the house. Most of the time, even our willpower and best intentions aren't enough to resist temptation. To save time, keep an ongoing shopping list taped to your refrigerator door. When you run out of something, write it down. This also saves unnecessary trips to the grocery store.

10. Store leftover food in see-through containers. To save s p a c e, use Lazy Susans for vitamins, spices, and canned goods. Put things that you don't use often such as the turkey roaster, 30 cup coffee urn, and ice cream maker in cupboards that are harder to reach.

11. Wean yourself from toxic cleaning chemicals. Replace them with products that won't harm you, your family, or the environment. Many of those familiar brands offer green products that are just as effective.

12. If your kitchen is looking a little tired, a fresh coat of paint can work wonders. So will an attractive lamp on the kitchen counter instead of overhead fluorescent lighting. A throw rug can improve the appearance of any floor. Hide the trash can under the sink. Get brooms and mops up off the floor. Hang an attractive poster on the wall and thin out the pictures and other stuff that may be cluttering your refrigerator.

Amount spent annually by McDonald's advertising its products: $800 million.

Amount spent annually by the National Cancer Institute promoting fruits and vegetables: $1 million.

– John Robbins

When we look deeply into our fears, we see that every fear is a fear of not having control.

– David Richo

FEAR

We've heard them all.

__The Acronym:__ False Evidence Appearing Real
__The Quote:__ There's nothing to fear except fear itself.
__The Thought:__ Thinking about fear is worse than fear itself.
__The Idea:__ Fear is a choice.
__The Truth:__ We're either in a state of love or fear.

Does reading about fear encourage us to jump off the edge into the unknown? Not usually. Even a steady mind, considered by some to be one of the most effective antidotes to fear, won't keep us out of the woods. But it is possible to ease our way into them. Since most people would rather cull their closets than heal their childhood wounds, let's begin with our material possessions. Because changing your mind about your stuff can also change your life.

At one end of the spectrum are the people who are taking sponge baths because their tub is filled with stuff, walking sideways through a maze of aisles, or saving foil candy wrappers for that possible art project. If you are clinging to your stuff like it's the last lifeboat on the Titanic, then you probably need professional help. Perfectionists sometimes fall into this category, especially if they are paralyzed with fear around not being able to do it "right."

Now, for those of you in the middle of the bell curve who are ready to get rid of stuff that you either don't like, use, or have outgrown but are feeling resistant, here's a suggestion. Remember that motivation follows action, not the other way around. This means that once you get going, anything can, and does, happen. Start with one small, non-threatening project like cleaning out your wallet, glove compartment, or bathroom drawer. You might discover that trashing the receipts from your billfold is all it takes to lure you down the road to a new lease on life.

The second suggestion is to shift your language. For example, use the word *release* instead of *giving up*, which may cause less stress. Sometimes, it's not the object that is hard to let go of, but our emotional attachment to it. So, allow yourself to feel the feelings around the "loss" and remember that you don't have to let go of anything if you aren't ready. Next week, even tomorrow, you may feel differently.

My third suggestion is to start affirming that you are recycling your unwanted stuff to someone who can use and/or enjoy what you no longer need but continue to hold on to. Giving back makes us feel good about ourselves and, as Henry Drumond says, "There is no happiness in having or getting, but only in giving." For you middle of the road group, the "I might need it someday" syndrome (someday is not a day of the week) will most likely be your biggest hurdle. But, it is your needing it someday that has caused you to have too much stuff.

Finally, at the far end of the spectrum are folks like me who don't want stuff - or least stuff that needs to be dusted. We can't wait to empty the trash, use up the last dollop of toothpaste, or look for any excuse to purge. It makes us feel better, even lighter. However, we aren't immune to our own arsenal of issues. Once, I tossed out a personalized license plate that I would now trade ten sushi dinners for. I can't find a patchwork floor length skirt that my grandmother spent months making for me. And then there are those sentimental things that I don't like but can't get rid of like the Shirley Temple doll my father gave me when

A practice in moving through fear. That's me cliff diving at Loch Raven Reservoir in Baltimore County, Maryland, 1988.

I was in the hospital, pictures of ancestors who I will never be able to identify, and the faded, crumbled corsage from my high school sweetheart.

We can't move forward if we don't know what's holding us back, so begin to notice how, what, where, who, and when you are resisting. Once you identify your fears and begin to understand the logic behind your resistance, it will make you less anxious and better equipped to effectively move through them.

This list of the ten most common fears can be used in all areas of your life:

1. *FEAR OF THE UNKNOWN:* Does the thought of scaling back bring up feelings of insecurity, especially if your future feels uncertain?

2. *FEAR OF BOREDOM:* Do you have an ongoing struggle with clutter that offers an element of excitement? Are you concerned that eliminating clutter will leave a void in your life?

3. *FEAR OF FACING REALITY:* Are you using possessions to distract yourself? Do they keep you from moving forward in your life?

4. *FEAR OF LETTING GO:* Does letting go of a tangible object feel like you are not only losing a part of yourself, but the memory attached to it?

5. *FEAR OF MAKING THE WRONG DECISION:* Do you procrastinate because you might give something away and find out later that it was a mistake? Do you believe that you might need it or that it could be valuable someday?

6. *FEAR OF EXPOSURE:* Do possessions give you a feeling of being insulated? Are you hiding behind them because you don't want the world to know what's underneath?

7. _FEAR OF LOSING CONTROL:_ If possessions belong to us, then we also have power over them. Do you use things to control others?

8. _FEAR OF LOSING PERSONAL IDENTITY:_ Possessions can be used to define who we are. Will having less make you less lovable to others? Do your belongings affect your status in the world?

9. _FEAR OF BETRAYAL:_ Giving away possessions that belonged to others can feel like you are betraying them. Does it feel like that person lives on in that thing? Will you be "hurting" the object, and them, if you can't find a good home for it? Where will it end up? And with whom?

10. _FEAR OF SCARCITY:_ Does the sight of empty s p a c e make you feel so uncomfortable that you have to fill it up with things? Does the thought of scaling back bring up memories of not having or not being enough?

Almost always it is the fear of being ourselves that brings us to the mirror.

– Antonio Porchia

One good reason for Feng Shui's current popularity is the obvious fact that our surrounding environment has been severely manipulated by man and, therefore, vastly changed from its natural origin. Another good reason for its rebirth is the legendary ability of the Feng Shui practitioner to bring good fortune to their clients through esoteric methods of adjusting the arrangements of their home or office.

– Lefty White

FENG SHUI

On my 54th birthday, I received a card from my friend Summer. In it she wrote, "I just love getting birthday cards with money…so, here's to the start of your birthday money magnet." Enclosed was a dollar bill, folded in half.

At the time, I had been reading a book about feng shui (pronounced "feng schway"). While the in-depth study includes more than I need to know, I was intrigued by one thing. It's about moving energy. The use of feng shui techniques activates, attracts, and optimizes the flow of energy, or chi, in the home and workplace.

In feng shui, the pa-kua (pronounced "par-kwar") is a grid used to determine the areas in your home that are connected to specific aspects in your life. The eight areas represented are wealth, fame, marriage, children, mentors, career, knowledge, and family. On the heels of Summer's birthday card, I dismissed any "mental clutter" as to why I thought it wouldn't work and decided to create a wealth center.

Referring to my feng shui book to determine the location of my wealth center, I was to stand inside my front door and look to the far diagonal corner of the house (if you have more than one level, choose any floor other than the basement; you can also do this for your office).

My wealth center was in the bedroom, right where a full length mirror already stood. Perfect. I learned that mirrors encourage chi. So does a hanging crystal, which I had in my office and promptly transferred over to my bedroom. I decided to add a sterling silver book mark and the dollar bill that Summer gave me. Other things that activate chi are hanging coins on the wall - a silent affirmation of greater abundance - and more light.

A fountain or fish bowl would also prove to be helpful because, in feng shui, water means wealth.

Within a week, I got a $500 check from someone who finally made good on a loan after two years. I received in the mail a coupon book with discounts for services that I could use - the local car wash, an oil change, and a facial. The next weekend, a furniture store owner offered to waive the delivery charge without my even having to ask her.

I began to keep a journal to track my prosperity. In the months that followed, the attendance at my yoga classes increased and my home staging business grew. I found $5 in the community washing machine and, three months later, $20 in the gutter near my home. Then there was the phone call announcing that I had won a drawing for a skin care treatment worth $300.

Other symbols of abundance include attracting people who have a wealth of information just when you need it, discovering that an item from your grocery list is on sale (instead of buying something *because* it is on sale), receiving a phone call from someone who makes you laugh, and reading an inspirational message that transforms your day.

I decided not to test the theory although, if you're a skeptic, I encourage you to do so. Stick a hamper piled with dirty clothes, a "catchall" chair, or stack a pile of papers and magazines in your wealth center and see what happens. After a while, you may notice a problem with cash flow, a lack of motivation to work, or an overall feeling of being in a rut.

A wealth center is sacred *s p a c e*, and creating it not only becomes a magnet for promoting balance, ease, and harmony, but also for attracting a better flow of energy into your life. Since abundance is our birthright, we only need to raise our awareness "antennae" to embrace it.

A dwelling should be not a retreat from s p a c e, but life in s p a c e.

– L. Hoholy-Nagy

If you want to know what people value,
look at how and where they spend their money.

– Pamela Glenconner

FINANCIAL SERENITY

It's one of the leading causes of psychological and emotional stress - debt. The once common sense practice of spending only what you have now seems revolutionary. But it's a challenge to neutralize our spending habits when we live in a society that not only encourages it, but also makes it impossible to resist, especially with easy terms and high limits carried by credit.

Over the years, I have discovered that it isn't money that complicates our lives, but what we believe it will do for us. While it can buy enjoyment, an easier lifestyle and a sense of freedom, it doesn't guarantee financial serenity. Not to be confused with being frugal, living cheaply, or feeling deprived, financial serenity affords us the opportunity to get in touch with what is really important.

Granted, once you begin to live more simply, your expenses will automatically be reduced. But there is shift in consciousness that also needs to happen. As a baby boomer, the messages that I received around money were confusing. My parents grew up in the Depression era where rationing was the norm. As a result, I had to save wrapping paper, clean my plate, and turn off the water when we were brushing our teeth - all good stuff for the environment - but along with my parents' scarcity consciousness came their drive to overconsume in an attempt to keep up with everyone else. Does this define financial serenity? I don't think so.

Money comes and goes. In my life, I've lived both ends of the spectrum and, even when I had plenty of money I was still in fear of not having enough. The illusion is that security comes from something outside of myself - my bank account, assets, the value of my possessions. Financial serenity comes from within. Abundance is my birthright and Spirit/God is the only thing that can prosper me. This doesn't mean that I go out and spend money that I don't have, lay around like a lounge lizard, or give up investing in my financial future. It means that I trust and, at the same time, do the footwork.

It's also important to distinguish between needs and wants. While needs are basic, wants are choices. Financial serenity is not about being stressed out about money. When I begin to feel that dark shroud of lack closing in, I remind myself that I have enough today - enough food, a comfortable place to live, warm clothes, and gas in my car. Although I may not have everything that I want, my needs have always been met. For me, this defines financial serenity.

Here are 20 ways to get you on the road to financial serenity:

1. Other than loans for big items such as a home, car, or education, clean up the financial clutter in your life. Spend only what you have using a debit card, checkbook, or cash. If you must have a credit card, pay it off every month.

2. Compulsive consumerism is an addiction. If your spending habits are out of control, seek professional help or join Debtors Anonymous. There, you will be able to connect with people who have been where you are and understand what you are going through. Overspending is a symptom of an underlying problem. Many of us spend way too much money on stuff that we don't need in order to fill what's missing inside.

3. Take some time to reflect on your spending habits. What kind of lifestyle are you buying, and does it align with your values? Energetically, does it serve you to acquire things if you can't afford them or don't need them? And, is your need for material gain more about the thrill of buying than owning?

4. Think before you buy. When in doubt, hold off. Ask yourself the following questions: Will having this particular thing

complicate or simplify your life? Can I afford it? How many hours will I have to work to pay for it? Do I really need it? Very often, if you wait 24 hours, you will find that the compulsion to have it diminishes.

5. Big box stores encourage over consumption. Unless you have a family of eight, you will probably spend more money than if you patronized a small store where you have the option to buy one of something.

6. Resist the temptation to buy something you don't need because it is on sale. Even if you only spend one dollar, it's not a bargain if you never use it.

7. You get what you pay for, so buy quality which will save you money in the long run.

8. If you have things in your home that are sitting around in their original packaging and not being used, you have not only wasted your money, but our natural resources as well.

9. Avoid reading coupon books, junk mail specials and newspaper & Internet ads for bargains. For now, toss the catalogs, which are filled with things that you wouldn't think to buy unless you saw them.

10. Advertising is seductive. Everyday we are being bombarded with advertising that encourages overspending such as buy two, get one free, limited supply, open an account and save 20%, buy now/pay later, call in the next 18 minutes and save $40.00, one day only sale.

11. Ways to cut back are to sell your health club membership if you aren't using it, get rid of your land line, drop your insurance premiums by raising your deductible, switch to CFL light bulbs, eat more meals at home, shop at thrift stores, clean out your rented storage space, drink water instead of sodas.

12. Money is energy that affords us the freedom to share it with others. Strive to make money a continuous flow of giving

and receiving. Withholding and hoarding it is fear-based energy that feeds a lack mentality.

13. When paying bills, shift your attitude to one of gratitude - specifically that you have the money to pay for them. When you find yourself grumbling about the high cost of heat and electricity, think about what the quality of your life would be without it.

14. What once bought a piece of candy can now give you a shift in consciousness. Every time you see a penny, pick it up and say, "I am prosperous." Use it as a symbol of your inner abundance by affirming it to the Universe.

15. Open yourself to inexpensive, simple pleasures that will make you feel more abundant. Buy fresh flowers. Use cloth napkins instead of paper. Drink sparkling water out of a wine glass.

16. Invest at least 10 percent of your income. Be consistent, and avoid moving around to beat the market. The key to success is knowing your risk tolerance. You want to feel comfortable with investments that are aggressive enough to outpace inflation. Pay yourself first; if you have an IRA, have a certain amount automatically taken out of your checking account every month. See your monetary assets as the gateway to a fabulous future instead of a fortress to be guarded. Financial serenity is not about putting so much money away that you can't enjoy it now.

17. Consider buying only necessities for one week. Then try it for one month. If you can do it for 30 days, then you can do it for 60.

18. Prosperity is a way of thinking, living, and being. Choose abundance and maintain your decision to have it. If you are creating for a "rainy day", then that is exactly what you will get.

19. On occasion, "splurge" consciously. Financial serenity is also about treating yourself to something luxurious because you are worth it!

20. Our lust for money will lessen when we begin to see our real assets through a spiritual lens - vibrant health, fulfilling relationships, inner peace, and creative work.

It is when you no longer feel the need for money that it will come. The feeling of needing money comes from the thought that you don't have enough, and so you will continue to create not having enough money. You are always creating, and when it comes to money, you are either creating the lack of it or the abundance of it.

– anonymous

Giving is a talent; to know what a person wants,
to know when and how to give it,
to offer it lovingly and well.

– Pamela Glenconner

GIFT GIVING

Looking back on my life, there are a handful of gifts that stand apart from the rest. This one arrived a few days before my 43rd birthday in 1994. Inside the card was the following message:

> Dear Kater,
>
> This card entitles you to a day of grateful friendship, laughter, and joy. My treat, anywhere you want to go. I am your personal chauffeur and companion.
>
> Love, Andrea

Andrea's gift - the gift of her time and the note that preceded it - has become the gold standard. On that magical, memorable birthday, we walked a labyrinth, shared lunch at a French bistro, browsed the neighborhood bookstore, and stopped by to see my grandmother.

Although there's a time and place for tangible* gift giving, this chapter is not about consumer spending. It is about remembering that there are few rewards more gratifying than being able to express our own unique Self through the art of gift giving. Each and every day, we have the ability to bring more meaning, pleasure, and satisfaction to others just by being who we are.

Too often, we fall victim to obligatory gift giving because the calendar says so. It feels like every time we turn around there's another holiday and, with it, one more gift to buy. It's time to clear the clutter of self-imposed guilt, duty, and "rightness."

Here are 15 intangible gift giving ideas:

1. The greatest gift that we can give to another human being is to be authentic, heart centered, and fully present.

2. Your gift to the world is living your soul's purpose. Share your skills, knowledge, and talents.

3. Since you wouldn't be here if it wasn't for them, acknowledge your parents by sending them a card on your birthday.

4. Give others the gift of hearing you say their first name, the most important word in the English language.

5. Instead of sending those seemingly obligatory Christmas, Kwaanza, or Hanukkah cards, send all the moms that you know a Mother's Day card...or choose from one of the many holidays throughout the year. These are unexpected treats that will leave a big deposit in your relationship accounts.

6. Share with people how much they mean to you either in person, by phone, or with a handwritten note. Leave little messages of appreciation around the house. If the thought of someone crosses your mind, pick up the phone, mail a card, or send an e-mail.

7. Make amends to those you have harmed. Otherwise, you are carrying around internal clutter.

8. Understanding others without judgment is one of the most precious gifts that you can give to another human being. Be honest without hurting others. Practice listening instead of giving advice.

9. Remember, if you don't allow others to give to you, then you are robbing them.

10. Sometimes, timing alone is all that it takes to turn a gift into a memorable one. After a death, avoid sending those predictable floral arrangements, chicken casseroles, or preprinted condolence cards. The most difficult times for the bereaved happen in the weeks after family, friends, and acquaintances are

gone. Invite the person out to lunch, pay them a visit, or send a handwritten note.

11. Offer to walk or spend time with pets that are left alone for long periods. If you have the time, spend it with the elderly, who often feel needy, vulnerable, and unlovable. They need connection, not things, and a few kind words can transform their day. As Mother Teresa said, "Every time you smile at someone, it is an action of love, a gift to that person, a beautiful thing."

12. Instead of arriving at the party with something that has to be dusted, send a handwritten thank you note instead. Nowadays, it may be the only one that the host receives, and you will be well remembered for the thought.

13. Intangible gifts include restaurant vouchers, movie coupons, housecleaning services, a certificate for car detailing or a body massage, concert tickets, a series of exercise classes, or a homemade dinner. If you are in a quandary as what to give someone whose interest, tastes, and style you're not familiar with, give them a gift certificate to a bookstore.

14. If you can afford the time, create a homemade coupon book with colored paper, stickers, and pens. This might include things that you will do for the other person - a foot and/or hand rub, a car wash, a trip to the ice cream store, a favorite meal, a "surprise" weekend, a night out at the movies, three hours of baby-sitting, dog walking, etc.

15. Transforming an ordinary tangible gift into an extraordinary one is easy and more heartfelt. For example, a ceiling fan that my parents gave me for a housewarming gift came with an electrician to install it. Fresh flowers are universally appreciated, especially if you bring them already in a vase. Or, pair a gift certificate for a pedicure, massage, or haircut with an offer of your time to babysit.

*When buying tangible gifts, support independent retailers, local businesses, and family-owned restaurants. Generally speaking, they are run by heart-driven, hard-working people who are out there swimming with the sharks. Even if something costs an extra dollar, it's a small price to pay for the opportunity to give back.

Should you choose to transition from less tangible to more intangible gift giving, begin to notice what happens - especially to you.

– unknown

If the only prayer you ever say in your life is "thank you," it will be enough.

– Meister Eckhart

Graces are those special gifts that break through our limits of mind, will, and heart. Grace expands our intellect by endowing us with intuitive wisdom. Grace expands our will by giving us a strength or courage we did not have before. Grace expands our hearts by making it possible to love rather than hate, to reconcile rather than retaliate, to show humility rather than hubris. Grace is the inner ally and guide, the motivating force of our spiritual practice.

– David Richo, from his book,
The Five Things We Cannot Change

GRACE

Our time together lasted a little over a decade. I can't say that she will ever speak to me again but, from her, I learned that forgiveness, compassion, and understanding are as close as my next breath.

I, being an introvert and earnest, found in her the perfect friend. She was a fizzy ball of energy, all 105 pounds of her, with spindly Olive Oyl limbs and poker straight, dark brown hair. A lighthearted person with a wonderful sense of humor and playful nature, she was like a little kid living in an adult body.

From the beginning, she and I hit it off, and together we shared common childhood experiences of having grown up in alcoholic homes. I confided in her and, very occasionally, she in me. Still, I felt like she had been so wounded that no one would ever be allowed past her dark, secret door.

I met her through my younger brother when they were dating. After two years, they were married and another "outlaw" joined the family. Throughout the nineties, during three difficult pregnancies on bedrest while my brother worked full time, my family supported her - bringing meals, hiring someone to help out, and running errands.

She was the kind of person that I couldn't stay mad at for long, and even though she betrayed me once I found it incredibly easy to forgive her. This was the first of several red flags and, as any good adult child of an alcoholic will understand, I chose to ignore them.

Then she and my brother split up. All of her repressed anger - toward her domineering mother, her beloved father who died when she was fourteen, and whatever else I didn't know about - emerged. My family, including my brother, became the scapegoat for her unresolved history and, as a result, she said and did some unspeakable things to us. I was crushed, even confused and, at times, unable to be consoled.

About a year went by when something happened that even a few months before would have been inconceivable. I was driving home from teaching a yoga class when an unexpected surge of love toward her washed through me. It was so powerful that I raced home to my computer and, as if taking dictation, wrote the following letter to her in less than 15 minutes:

Dear Annie,

For whatever reason, while driving home today, I was intuitively guided to write you. There is no motivation other than Divine Guidance.

I am sad that you and my brother are getting divorced and that it has been difficult to work things out amicably for the sake of your three children. I feel burdened by the enormous pain that this must be causing you, and them. It hurts me to think of you having to raise them single-handedly while you work outside of the home. I am also sad for any pain and suffering you are experiencing.

What I miss the most about not having you in my life is that adorable, beautiful little child inside that I met over a decade ago. You always seemed to have a knack for bringing out the kid in me, and I so appreciated that all these years.

Even though we are all on our own path in life, these are my wishes for you. From this day forward, I wish for you freedom from hurt, anger, and suffering. I wish for you abundant love and health. And, most of all, I wish for you a life filled with peace and happiness.

Now, it didn't matter if the letter was going change Annie's mind about me, or if she would receive it, or even read it. What mattered is that I had been given the gift of grace - which was the ability to forgive, feel compassion, and finally understand.

Forgiveness, I knew, was not about forgetting, but about letting go of the hurt. Understanding came through from remembering that Annie, like all of us, was walking her own path and doing her best. And, compassion is rooted in the truth that we are spiritual beings having a human experience.

I've heard it said that love is our finest human grace. Sometimes grace comes to us when we least expect it. Although it doesn't hurt to ask, it's that much sweeter if we don't. Grace is God's empowering presence filling those empty s p a c e s inside, allowing us to remember who we are and to discover what is truly important - love, friends, family, friends. Grace is the journey of our soul.

Rain is grace; rain is the sky condescending to the earth; without rain, there would be no life.

– John Updike

They're not the best at what they do,
they're the only ones that do what they do.

– from a Grateful Dead bumper sticker

I may be going to hell in a bucket,
but at least I'm enjoying the ride.

– Grateful Dead lyric

You aren't going to learn
what you don't want to know.

– Grateful Dead lyric

GRATEFUL DEAD

This story is a lesson in never judging a book by its cover, a story about a group of musicians who broke every rule in the music industry and how they became one of the top grossing bands of all time.

. . . .

The Grateful Dead came into my life at the start of their 1985 fall tour, in September. Already, they had been around for twenty years. Over the span of many moons, it was my friend Jason who wouldn't give in to my resistance to see them.

"Just come and check them out," he would say.

"Maybe."

"What have you got to lose?"

"I don't know."

A few months later, I couldn't say no when he offered me a free Red Rocks concert ticket, a place to stay in Boulder, and cheap airfare to Colorado.

"Okay," I finally told him, "I'll go."

. . . .

We flew, Jason and I, nonstop to Denver from Baltimore. Upon our arrival at the airport, Jason's brother Stephen and their friend Marc were there to pick us up. As the four of us hiked across the parking lot to the car, they filled Jason in on every detail of the last two shows.

"Did they play *Eyes*?" I asked.

Stephen, knowing that I had never been to a concert, looked surprised.

"Yeah, day before yesterday."

"Bummer."

I loved *Eyes of the World*. At the time, it was the only other song that I was familiar with besides *Truckin'*. I knew *Eyes* from a bootleg tape that Stephen had given me a few years back.

As we veered out of mainstream America from the airport terminal toward The Red Rocks Amphitheater in Morrison, Colorado, I was about to step into another world, one known as a Grateful Dead concert.

I, like many others in my generation, knew of the Grateful Dead. Most of us heard that they bombed at Woodstock, not to mention they had a name that took some getting used to. Their first two albums, *Historic Dead* and *Vintage Dead* were flops. Then, in 1973, their beloved keyboard player, Pigpen, died from cirrhosis of the liver.

Already, a few miles before Red Rocks Park, people were standing by the side of the road holding cardboard signs that read "I need a miracle."

"So, what does that mean?" I asked Jason.

"They're looking for a ticket to get in. It's also the name of one of their songs."

Others, also looking for a ticket, held one index finger tirelessly in the air. Dead shows, Jason told me, were always sold out.

Three generations of Deadheads, from left: Jason, Barry, me and Barry's son, Matt.
1988

The story of the Grateful Dead began on New Year's Eve in 1963. Bob Weir and a friend dropped in on Jerry Garcia who was teaching banjo lessons at a music store in Palo Alto. When his student didn't show up, Garcia and Weir started to jam. By the end of the night, they decided to put a jug band together.

The band - known as Mother McCree's Uptown Jug Champions - included Jerry Garcia, Bob Weir, and Ron "Pigpen" McKernan, among other members. (Garcia met Pigpen, a harmonica player, when he would occasionally sit in on a blues band called the Zodiacs.) Mother McCree's stayed together for almost a year. Garcia would later say, "We'd work out various kinds of musically funny material. It was like a musical vacation to get on stage and have a good time."

By the spring of 1965, Garcia (on lead guitar and vocals), Pigpen (harmonica, keyboards, and vocals), and Weir (rhythm guitar and vocals) decided to assemble another band, calling themselves the Warlocks. They found Bill Kreutzman, a drummer who also taught music at the store in Palo Alto. By summer, Phil Lesh came on board as their bass player, followed by Mickey Hart who joined them in 1967.

The Warlocks played at parties (known as "Acid Tests,") given by Ken Kesey who wrote *One Flew Over the Cuckoo's Nest*. Kesey headed what became known as The Merry Pranksters, a group of people who dropped LSD, which was legal at that time. Kesey discovered it when he volunteered for a government program that conducted experiments with the drug.

The Warlocks became the so-called "house band" for the Acid Tests in and around the San Francisco area in 1965 and 1966. As Garcia put it, "We had no significance. We weren't famous. Nobody came to the Acid Test to see us, particularly. We got to play or not play, depending on how we felt. We could play anything we could think of, which meant we didn't have any constraints on our performance. We didn't have to be good, or even recognizable. We had an opportunity to visit highly experimental places under the influence of highly experimental chemicals before a highly experimental audience. It was ideal. And that was something we got to do long enough to get used to it."

It was during the Acid Test era that they finally found their new name - *Grateful Dead*. The story goes that Jerry Garcia opened an Oxford dictionary and found grateful dead. The juxtaposition of those two words had enough shock value that it made the name noticeable. As Robert Hunter said, "Once heard, the name is not forgotten."

On that hot, sun bleached day at Red Rocks, I saw every imaginable vehicle sporting license plates from all over the country. Fans, known as "Deadheads," came on motorcycles, in limousines, U-Haul trucks, old school buses converted into homes on wheels, even on horseback. Some hitchhiked, using tattered signs to get there. Just beyond the entrance to the park, I noticed two guys pushing their battery dead Volvo through the gate and off to the side where it was abandoned - at least for now.

We were told that the parking lots at the top were full, so we parallel parked along one side of the long winding incline to the amphitheater and started hiking up.

Once we made our way to the top, we split up in pairs. While Stephen and Marc headed for the "Will Call" window, Jason and I hung out in the parking lot.

"Welcome to the show before the show," he said, laughing.

As we walked around, pushing our way through the crowd, a symphony of bootlegs could be heard from numerous car tape decks. Fans pulled little red wagons filled with beer, sodas, and bottled water for sale. Some got around on skateboards. Small clusters of Deadheads played hackysack, while dogs with bandanas around their necks chased frisbees.

"The area up ahead where you see all the vendors is Shakedown Street," Jason told me, "named after one of their albums."

Shakedown Street was festive, friendly, and buzzing with activity. Row after row of blankets were laid out on the ground, covered with candles, clothing, incense, posters, jewelry, and bumper stickers for sale. Women with painted faces carried wicker baskets filled with beautiful, long stemmed red roses. Homemade food, mostly vegetarian, was served from makeshift kitchens in the back of Volkswagen buses.

"By the way, the food is much better in the parking lot than it is inside," Jason cautioned me.

Almost never being able to resist food, I promptly bought a homemade black bean burrito made to order. It was a delicious mix of mashed beans, salsa, lettuce, grated cheddar, and sweet onions - all for a buck.

Jason told me the parking lots become camping grounds because many people are on the road with the band. Selling food and merchandise is big business for those who follow the Dead. Being a Tourhead is a lifestyle and, with three to four tours a year, many fans turn a nice profit on their wares.

"Want to buy a homemade chocolate chip cookie?" a soft voice with a baby strapped to her back asked me.

The cookie was huge, the size of a saucer. I picked one out and downed it on the spot.

The sound of ankle bell bracelets and the aroma of patchouli oil and pot threaded through the air as we began to shuffle through the growing crowd toward the ticket gate. While I stopped to check out some crystals, Jason bought a "Women Are Smarter" bumper sticker, another name of a song.

Once we cleared the ticket gate and spilled out into the amphitheater, I was struck by the breathtaking views. The 9,000 seat Red Rocks Amphitheater was built high on a hill overlooking the foothills. It had huge slabs of rock - as tall as a four-story building - on either side of the stage where one could peer out into the world beyond while listening to the music. Playing in the Colorado Rockies was the perfect spot for the Dead to funnel their songs about outcasts, gamblers, and others on the road less traveled.

"Hey, Jason!"

He jerked his head around to see where the voice was coming from.

"Down here," she said, waving her arms fluidly in the air.

"That's my friend, Jill. You may have met her. She lives in Baltimore."

I shook my head.

As we descended our way through the puppy piles of people, Jason told me that Jill was a seasoned second-generation Deadhead. When she was a baby, her parents strapped her to their backs and went to Dead shows in and around the San Francisco Bay area. At three years old, she knew many of their lyrics.

"Hi, I'm Jill," she said, extending her warm, sweaty palm my way from a seat in the second row.

"Great spot," Jason said, giving her a bear hug.

"It better be. I've been here since 9 this morning."

While she and Jason chatted, I watched her finish making an ankle bracelet out of multi-colored beads.

When Jason felt the energy building among the waiting crowd, he turned to Jill and told her that maybe we would catch her after the show.

"Sounds great."

Then, Jill handed me the ankle bracelet she had made.

"For you," she offered, cradling it in the cup of both hands.

I slipped a sandal off, tied it around my ankle, and thanked her.

With that, Jason and I turned and made the climb to our seats - about midway up - where Stephen (who looked just like Jerry Garcia) was waiting for us. I heard Jason ask him where Marc was.

"He had to make a phone call."

I sat down and looked around.

It was obvious that Dead shows were about connecting with others and having fun. Welcome hugs and outbursts of joy could be seen and heard throughout the crowd - a tribe of people lost and found. I was already hooked, deciding that this is how I would have imagined the Summer of Love in 1967.

Then, just as Marc stepped over me to get by, the band came out and immediately everyone stood up. Through the sounds of whistles, clapping, and cheering, Jason pointed out each band member on stage.

"That's Bob Weir in the middle. Phil Lesh is on the left. The two drummers, Bill Kreutzman and Mickey Hart, are in the back. Brent Mydland is all the way over to the right, next to Jerry.

I fixed my eyes on Jerry.

"For years, Jerry stood on the left. Then one day, for whatever reason, he switched to the other side. Except for Brent, who replaced Pigpen after his death, all of the band members are original."

Clearly, their following is legendary. Some fans refer to themselves as closet Deadheads and, in "real" life, go underground to protect their image and/or career. Although often typecast, not all Deadheads are burned out hippies wandering around aimlessly from gig to gig. I looked over at Jason, Stephen, and Marc - a medical student, a Ph.D. in philosophy, and a dentist, respectively.

As they were warming up, Jerry broke a guitar string. While he was backstage, the band played *The Star Spangled Banner.*

Stephen cracked up, saying, "I think we just got the bonus up front."

Already, I had witnessed the predictably unpredictable magic of the Grateful Dead.

While we waited for Jerry to come back, I noticed a slew of microphones behind the soundboard area.

I nudged Marc, pointing.

"Tapeheads. They have special tickets to get into a designated taping section."

"So that explains all of the bootlegs," I said.

Stephen jumped on it. "As far as I know, they're the only band that allows it."

Jason's brother, Stephen, could have been Jerry Garcia's double. This photograph was taken in 1983 with his daugher, Raisin.

Finally, Jerry came out and they opened the show with *Mississippi Half Step*, a playful, country fiddle tune with some jazz thrown in.

Part of the Grateful Dead phenomenon is their ability to improvise. Their repertoire includes psychedelic, rhythm and blues, bluegrass, and rock & roll. With well over 2,000 shows in 30 years, they never repeated a song list twice or played one exactly the same. For them, "rehearsals" were their live concerts, just like they were at the Acid Tests back in the mid-sixties.

"When we get onstage, we really want to be transformed from ordinary players to extraordinary ones, like forces of a larger consciousness. So maybe it's that seat-of-the-pants shamanism that keeps the audience coming back and that keeps it fascinating for us, too," Jerry was quoted as saying.

Interesting, however, is that their format rarely wavered. There were two sets, about an hour each, with a 45 minute intermission. *Drums and s p a c e* were always played in the second set. At the end, there was one encore, maybe two. They only spoke to announce the break.

"We'll be right back," Bob Weir would say.

Beyond that, anything could happen.

At Red Rocks, most of the deadheads were either dancing in front of their seats or "twirling" in the narrow aisles. Some fans walked up and down the steps selling Dead-inspired art printed on tee shirts, most of which they had designed themselves.

The band continued on, playing *Minglewood, Be Women, Easu, Loser,* and *Dupree's*, the first song that Robert Hunter and Jerry Garcia wrote together. Before they went to break, they electrified the crowd with *Saturday Night.*

I decided to get up, find a bathroom, and walk around. On the way back to my seat, I stopped to take in the view of downtown Denver. It stood motionless, a welcome contrast to the frenzy of activity going on around me.

Where else, I thought to myself, can one go around looking weird and not feel judged? Here, people can be who they are or who they want to be. No one seemed to care if men were dressed in skirts or that women were breast feeding their babies or that little kids were running around half naked.

I looked to my left, where a young couple were standing with a child nestled contentedly between their legs. The kid, who was wearing a tie-dyed dress, was already being groomed for Deadheadom. I thought of Jill and wondered what it was like to be raised by hippy parents.

This photo was taken at a Dead show in Tempe, Arizona on August 18, 1987. To keep his hair stiff, he used shellac.

To my right, I noticed a man, probably in his late forties, leaning against the ledge. His hair, the color of ground flax seeds and parted down the middle, cascaded to his shoulders in soft waves. Except for a small hoop in his left ear, he could have been Jesus reincarnate.

He had a peaceful, wise old soul aura about him.

In an attempt to complement his energy and increase my odds of hooking into a conversation, I approached him cautiously.

"This place is just amazing," I said.

He looked my way and smiled.

"First time at Red Rocks?"

I nodded. "Also, my first Dead show."

"You picked a great venue."

When I asked him if he had ever been there before, he said yes, in 1978, the first time they played at Red Rocks.

"Wow. So, how long have you been following them?"

"Since the mid-sixties. Actually, I grew up in the Bay area."

I told him that I had been born on the wrong coast, that I should have been born in San Francisco, too.

He looked at me with curiosity but didn't comment. Then he shook my hand and introduced himself.

"Hi, my name's Ryan."

Ryan went on to tell me he was in the Haight the day the Dead gave a free concert in the spring of 1968.

"It was rumored that they didn't have a permit, so they just set up and played in the street."

"Were there tons of people there?"

"It was packed."

"How cool is it that their fans are allowed to tape their concerts," I said, feeling proud to have at least some inside knowledge of the band.

"They understand that in order to keep something you have to give it away."

I told him that my father would come home from his A.A. meetings and say the same thing.

"Instead of putting their energy in promotion, they would rather attract," he said. "They play music for the pure pleasure of doing what they love. If you like them, great. If you don't, that's okay, too."

The crowd was clapping in unison now, prompting people to return to their seats in anticipation for the second set.

"Remember The Monterey Pop Festival in '67?" he asked.

"I know that it put Janis Joplin and Jimi Hendrix on the map."

"Those two were incredible ... no one had ever seen anyone like them before. They blew the audience away. It was the first venue that Hendrix played when he came to America from England."

Ryan was a walking rock 'n roll encyclopedia.

"Who else was there?" I asked.

He rattled them off, one by one.

"Jefferson Airplane, Simon and Garfunkel, the Byrds, The Mamas and the Pappas...they were fabulous...Country Joe and the Fish, the Who. Anyway, after the festival was over, the Dead held a free concert at a nearby college for the thousands who weren't able to get in."

"No wonder people love them."

"That's the other thing." he said. "They want to stay connected to their fans. I remember the *Skull and Roses* album. When it was released in 1971, they not only included their address, but a message to Deadheads. They even have their own mail order business."

Just then, everyone cheered as the band came back out.

Moving away from the wall where we were leaning, he looked over at me and said, "No matter how much anyone knows about the Dead, it's almost impossible to define them."

And, with that, he turned to walk down the concrete ramp in his battered Birkenstocks and khaki shorts. I noticed that on the back of his white tee shirt, printed in black letters, was "Have a Grateful Day".

The band had already warmed up and opened with *Shakedown Street*, a disco "style" song with some rhythm and blues added. The crowd went nuts. I noticed that Stephen was writing the name of the song on the back of his concert ticket.

As they played, fans were bouncing multi-colored balloons into the air. Occasionally, someone would raise a spray bottle and pump mists of cool water into the hot summer air, giving relief to anyone in its path.

Then they played *Uncle John's Band*, a country-style signature song about people pulling together through challenging times. About halfway into the second set, everyone but Mickey Hart and Bill Kreutzman left the stage, prompting many fans to sit down in their seats.

"Okay, educate me. What's going on now," I said to Jason.

"We call it *drums and s p a c e*, a little drumming and percussion show of their own."

Even though it is nirvana for those on LSD or marijuana, it was my least favorite part of the show.

After what seemed like an eternity, Jerry, Bob, Phil, and Brent returned to the stage, moving right into *Mr. Fantasy>Hey Jude>Truckin'>Comes a Time>Lovelight*. All were crowd pleasers, including their two encores *Johnny B. Goode* and *Baby Blue*, a Rolling Stones tune.

When the concert was over, the four of us made our way out of the amphitheater and slowly descended the hill to our car.

"It will take all night to clear everyone out of the park," Stephen told me.

"You mean the show after the show?"

Before we drove off, Jason slapped the "Women Are Smarter" bumper sticker on the back of Stephen's rental car.

The next morning, most vendors would be packed and on their way to the next three shows in Oakland, California. Jason and Stephen flew back to Baltimore while Marc drove me to Colorado Springs where I would visit my cousin for a few days.

Over the next ten years, I would go on to see the Grateful Dead thirty-five times in seven states across the country. Like the band itself, everything surprised me and nothing surprised me. In Washington, D.C., I saw a woman with a full-grown boa constrictor coiled around her body like a bracelet, wrapped twice around her waist, then up her back and over her shoulder with its head resting motionless on her right breast. Then there was the seventy-five-year-old man sitting behind me at a show in Long Beach California who had discovered the Dead in his sixties. And, a "career" highlight was the time that I heard *Eyes of the World* for the first time in concert, having waited five years after missing it by two days at Red Rocks.

By the late 1980's, the band hit the mainstream with the release of their album *In the Dark*. The number of Deadheads was growing younger. In *People* magazine, Peter Jennings was photographed at a Dead show with his two teenage kids. As their popularity continued to climb the charts, so did the venues. More and more, they were touring large stadiums and arenas.

In 1995, they celebrated their thirtieth year. The spring tour kicked off at The Spectrum in Philadelphia, where all the buzz was around hearing Phil Lesh play *Unbroken Chain* after twenty-three years. I can still see the fans standing in long lines at the pay phones, waiting to call their friends with the late breaking news.

However, there were problems on that tour. One fan was struck by lightning in Washington, D.C. Then, on television, I watched in disbelief when a group of fans without tickets stormed through the gates outside of Indianapolis, Indiana - a first. In St. Louis, a deck collapsed on 100 people seeking cover from a rainstorm. I wasn't immune either; Terry and I had an argument after a show in D.C.

When the tour ended at Soldier Field in Chicago on July 9, 1995, Jerry Garcia checked into rehab. One month later, on my father's birthday - August 9 - my sister called from California to tell me that he had died.

That night, across the country, candlelight vigils were held. *Time* magazine featured Jerry on its August 21st cover. In it,

President Clinton was quoted as saying on MTV that, "Garcia had a great gift. And he even wound up putting out that line of ties. He had great ties...I went around wearing Jerry Garcia ties and gave them away to people. I was very sad when he died."

The following week, Jerry's memorial service was held in Golden Gate Park. A year after his death, everyone except Phil Lesh resumed touring under the band's new name "The Other Ones." They filled a void for Deadheads, but it would never be the same without Jerry. In 2003, when Phil Lesh returned to the group, they called themselves "The Dead."

Today, their legacy lives on in bootleg tapes, CDs, and their ongoing support for such charitable organizations as the Rainforest Action Network and Cultural Survival. Not only did they model the law of attraction, but the value of being authentic, and that giving is receiving tenfold. On a more personal note, every show gave me the opportunity to experience the peace and love generation of my youth and, in a strange sort of way, I was able to make good on my sheltered, adolescent years growing up.

. . . .

On a mild night in June of 1995, Terry and I arrived on a commuter train for a Dead show in Washington D.C. I remember they played a killer *Truckin'* in the second set. After the concert was over, we hung out in the parking lot for a while. There, we could see the trains come and go along the crest of the hill every fifteen minutes or so. On that dark, overcast night, the sight of those trains illuminated by fluorescent light and filled with Deadheads wearing every tie-dye color in the rainbow literally took my breath away.

Then, wearing the beaded ankle bracelet that Jill had given me at Red Rocks a decade before, I boarded the train that would take me home from my last Grateful Dead show.

Sometimes, there's nothing left to do but smile, smile, smile.

– Grateful Dead lyric

Pain is your best friend. It is infinitely more honest with you than pleasure. Despite what you might think, the painful experiences you have had benefit you far more than the pleasurable ones, even though most of us spend our lives trying to duck and hide from them. But when you can center yourself and be open to look pain dead in the eye, then you have transcended the limits of your ego and this humanity. It is then that you enter into the possibility of becoming a great being.

— Swami Chentanananda

GRIEF

t's usually the fastest road to healing, yet the one we most avoid – that of feeling emotional pain. Unresolved grief comes at a price, not only to ourselves but to those around us. It can lead to depression, passive-aggressive behavior, and the inability to resolve the past. Nikki Stern, whose husband died on 9/11, said that grieving people are vulnerable and susceptible to any and all opportunities to ease their pain. My inability to deal with grief was as debilitating as the substances I used to numb it for over three decades.

For most of my life, anger was my emotion of choice. It felt safe and strong, a good match for my tomboy nature with its masculine and powerful energy. Being mad not only got me noticed around our house growing up, but it was an effective smokescreen for the loneliness, powerlessness, and frustration that I was feeling.

In all fairness to anger, however, it did serve me in some positive ways. It protected me, forced me to make different choices, and effectively channeled my fear, worry, and guilt. But underneath it all was a profound sadness that left me feeling vulnerable, out of control, and messy. While I don't like messy, crying does allow me to let go and accept what is.

Repressed emotions run in my family. My great grandmother used to sit by the dining room window, rocking in her chair, and swallow her solace in the passages of the Bible. I only saw my grandmother cry once, a faint whimper that was triggered by the daunting task of having to downsize from a four bedroom house to a two bedroom apartment. Then there is my mother who hates to cry, claiming that it gives her a migraine for days after. For me the seeds were planted well, and I would go on

My best male friend, Stuart. This picture was taken two months before he was killed by a drunk driver in 1980.

to carry the baton of unexpressed grief, smiling through the daily pages of my angry life to conceal the pain.

Often, I think about my friend Stuart who was killed by a drunk driver on Cold Bottom Road, about 25 miles north of Baltimore. Tragically, his life ended in 1980, the same year that M.A.D.D. was organized by Candy Lightner, whose 13-year-old daughter, Cari, was killed by a hit and run drunk driver on a suburban California street. I didn't want to feel the deep-seated sadness of losing Stuart, so I chose instead to stay angry at myself for never having returned the phone message he left me three weeks before his death.

Holding onto anger keeps me stuck and, for years, I did so because I believed it would somehow change my reality. For example, the older and more dependent my beloved grandmother became, the angrier I got. It wasn't the adult who was mad, but the ten year old kid inside who knew that her death was going to leave a terrible void, and I couldn't bear to feel the pain.

Grief work is an emotional and spiritual experience, not a mental exercise that I can think my way out of. When I finally stopped drinking, the abysmal well of sadness felt like more than I could handle. I remember being afraid that once I started crying that I would never be able to stop. And yet, that was the very thing I needed to do - to just start and trust that God wouldn't give me more than I could handle.

There are times when I don't know which is worse - losing a loved one suddenly or slowly, over time. After my father was diagnosed with lung cancer, his hair began to fall out and his energy waned, followed by his inability to write and, finally, walk the stairs. Dad's choice to leave this world in bits and pieces was his gift to me. For seven months, it allowed me to grieve in layers as he steadily faded away.

Sometimes, grieving the loss of someone I love is less about the person and more about the way they made me feel or what the relationship represented. When Terry and I separated after thirteen years of marriage, the bigger loss was the companionship, the things that we shared, and our day to day routine. Ultimately, the deeper pain came down to missing our "us-ness" more than him.

Through the years, I have discovered that the nature of grieving has many faces including confusion, elusiveness, and unpredictability. For example, I couldn't have imagined that seeing the movie *Boys Don't Cry* (the true story of Teena Brandon, a woman masquerading as a man, who was raped, beaten and murdered) would prompt me to sob on and off for three days. Watching my father suffer at a sloth's pace was no easy task, but to have Stuart suddenly ripped from my life from that car accident, was somehow harder to endure. And, the inability to grieve the loss of my grandmother, Marnie, for ten years after she died still remains a mystery.

When I push through the distractions and face my pain head on, it feels like pulling a plug on my internal drain, allowing the energy to flow through me like a fresh mountain spring. Although I am not hard wired to cry easily, grief work reminds me that I am enough, if for no other reason than I can feel. Carter Cooper's last words to his mother, Gloria Vanderbilt, before he jumped off of her 14th floor Manhattan terrace, were "Will I ever feel again?"

In the higher realms, we move through life and interact in relation to feeling. The ability to feel pain is essential to our well-being and survival. Grief reminds us that we have lived fully, and every opportunity to do so clears more *s p a c e*, restores emotional balance, and moves mountains.

We are healed of a suffering
only by experiencing it to the full.

– Marcel Proust

God, grant me the serenity to accept the things I cannot change, the courage to change the things I can, and the wisdom to know the difference.

— Reinhold Niebuhr

INTERNAL CLUTTER

Here are some examples of the less obvious, more insidious forms of clutter that we carry around:

MENTAL

Illusions

Toxic thinking

Avoidance

Old beliefs

Living in the past or the future

Ego

Self-doubt and criticism

Unrealistic Expectations

Regrets

Shoulds

Procrastinating

Boredom

EMOTIONAL

Unresolved grief and anger

Fear

Anxiety

Guilt and shame

Resentment

Blame

Suspicions

VERBAL

Inability to speak our truth

Negative self-talk

Offensive language

VISUAL

Looking at material clutter

Too much information on Web pages

Wordy text

PHYSICAL

Illness

Stress

Consuming toxic food

Obsession with weight

Feeling lethargic

Depression

Affects of sexual abuse

Chronic pain

SPIRITUAL

Arrogance

Low self-esteem

Lack of faith

Feeling separate from others

Inability to trust

Everything is meant to be let go of so that the soul may stand in unhampered nothingness.

– Meister Eckhart

Journal writing is a voyage to the interior.

– Christina Baldwin

JOURNALING

Even as a self-proclaimed writer, it took years to integrate a daily journaling practice into my life. I always know when a habit has been installed because it will gnaw at me if I haven't done it for a few days. But even though this writer will never fall in love with journaling, I keep doing it. Sometimes, my mind is like a sieve and when I go back to look at what I've written, it's those precious details that make it worth every second of my time.

If you want to journal but don't have time, break it down. Write about important events, interesting places, or people who have inspired you. For example, keep detailed notes when you travel, which will serve to enrich the pictures in your photo albums. As a writer, I like to take detailed notes at workshops, seminars, or lectures which always add richness to a story.

Journaling my experiences also keeps the memories alive, like the day that I took the train from Baltimore to New York to visit Ground Zero, 22 days after the terrorist attacks. I wrote down sensory details, like the eerie absence of city noise. Only the sound of the bulldozers working 24/7 could be heard clearing away the horror of that Tuesday morning. I remember running my fingers over the flour-like dust that covered everything. And the air, so thick with the smell of cement that my throat was irritated for days.

Overall, documenting my daily thoughts, feelings, and behavior helps to clarify them. Writing allows me to see where I was, what patterns are still there, and how far I have come. It affirms that I really am moving forward in my life.

So, in honor of journaling, I share with you the following story. Of all my writing efforts, I am most grateful for having given myself the *s p a c e* to record this one.

. . . .

A few years after my father died, during a downpour of rain one morning, I was rummaging through my tax files in search of an old receipt. When I couldn't find it, I started purging paper from my office. One thing led to another and, before I knew it, I was reorganizing my bookshelves.

I began to take everything off, starting with the top two shelves. Pads of paper, business cards, packing tape, and envelopes came down until all that was left were dust balls and papers clips.

Then, tackling the bottom shelf from left to right, I starting clearing off telephone books, 3-ring binders, and magazines. About halfway across, hidden behind the books, was a small stack of papers, stapled together and folded in half.

I opened up the 9" x 11" parchment papers.

"Oh, my God," I said out loud, then mumbled under my breath, "Out of sight, out of mind."

I got up to toast a slice of rice bread. By now, the rain was pelting against our floor to ceiling windows. While standing motionless in front of the toaster oven, I tried to absorb what I had just found. Then I went back into my office to get the papers.

I returned to the kitchen, slathered the toast with crunchy peanut butter, walked into the den, and plopped down on the sofa. After clearing my throat and taking a bite, I started to read the first of nine handwritten pages, covering the last week of my father's life, from May 5-12, 1996.

I thought about the events of that last week. I remembered the exact time that he died and how I felt when he took his last breath. I can still see him, as if it happened yesterday, staring out his bedroom window with tears running down his cheeks as he watched his grandchildren frolic on the hill behind the house. And I will never forget watching my older brother and his family - who had to leave the day before he died - say good-bye to him for the last time.

I looked out the window again. The tops of the trees were bending like limp celery against the wind. Poplars are brittle, and we had several of them on our property. Now, a tree toppling over on our house could serve as a metaphor for the memory of my father's last week crashing down on me.

I ripped off another chunk of peanut butter toast and kept reading. Midway through the journal, I realized how much I had forgotten. There were the soothing words that Dad used to ease my pain, the unexpected ways in which he expressed gratitude, and his ability to be selfless. I was also reminded of just how much he made me laugh, what he ate the night before he died, and his last words to me. I turned another page, and then another, each page breathing life back into those last, final days.

I put the stack of papers down and looked out at the rainstorm, now beginning to wane. The light was beginning to brighten over the pond, splashing the treetops in pure white gold. A few minutes later, a rainbow appeared - a timely reminder of my father.

With tears in my eyes, I picked up the journal again and held it close to my heart. It had been hiding behind the telephone books, 3-ring binders, and magazines for over five years. Clearly, this was a story waiting to be found and, like life and death itself, it too had come full circle - beginning and ending on a Sunday.

<u>Sunday, May 5, 1996</u>

It will exactly take 55 minutes to drive from my gated community to my parents' gated community - without traffic. Even though it's not far enough to warrant an overnight, this time I pack enough clothes for two nights and three days.

It is 4:30 p.m. when I make the final turn into their complex. With my car locked and gear in tow, I walk up to my parents' red brick townhouse and step through the front door. Immediately, the smell of Mother's freshly baked bread draws me into the kitchen where she is preparing supper. Her food will be delicious, as it always has been.

I can hear the television in the den, just off the kitchen. That's where Dad is. Things around here seem normal, except that they aren't. My father has been sick for months, and is dying.

Like me, Mother likes to cook alone so I join Dad on the sofa, where we talk with the noise of the television in the background - nothing too deep, just idle chit chat. Predictably, my mother and father will eat before watching *60 Minutes*, something that they have done for the past 25 years.

I begin to feel nervous sitting on the sofa next to him. With Dad, one on one conversation - unless it's light or humorous - has never felt comfortable. Talking with my father about "what ifs," or feelings, or the past is off limits. However, tonight is different. There is something I want to ask him, at the right moment of course.

I get up to get a glass of water from the kitchen. When I come back, Dad has turned the television off. This is my cue and, not wanting to waste any time, I sit down on the sofa, take my shoes off, and turn toward him.

"Dad," I blurt out, then pausing long enough to think that if I'm going to chicken out, then here's my chance.

"Yes, honey," he answers, taking a swallow of something I know is nonalcoholic.

I put my feet up on the coffee table and cross my arms.

"I'm curious," I say, feeling myself about to stumble, "what do you think...I mean, do you think about dying?"

While I exhale the air from my lungs fully, Dad takes another swig of his beverage.

Then, he takes my hand and, without missing a beat, says, "I think about how rich and blessed I am, and you are a part of that."

I couldn't help but think about my father's childhood. He was born into a staunch, conservative, German background, the second of four children. His father was a pharmacist by trade and a hillbilly at heart. Dad's mother, a homemaker, loved and appreciated the finer things in life. Obvious to many was the fact that Dad's younger brother, who was breast fed until the age of 5, was the favored child. This drove my father to be an overachiever in order to win the attention, approval, and affection of his parents. He rarely talked about his childhood, although I am quite sure that he raised us the same way - with a big stick, a sharp tongue, and a look that could move mountains.

Now, age has softened the edges around my father and I am reduced to tears by his response to my question. But, that's my father who, like his father, kept everything inside. Now, for the first time in our relationship, my father and I are crying together.

After dinner, Mother washes the dishes while I clean the stove and countertops. This time next week, Dad will be gone. Before heading to bed with my book, *The Power of Decision* by Raymond Charles Barker, I massage his feet. Then, at 7:00 p.m., I leave them to their beloved *60 Minutes*.

<u>Monday, May 6</u>

I am awakened by a soft tap on my bedroom door. Mother tells me that Dad is on his hands and knees in excruciating pain, having gotten up to go to the bathroom in the early hours of the morning.

"Could you help me get him up off the floor?"

"Sure, Mom. Give me a minute to get some clothes on."

I cringe, remembering how athletic Dad was. During World War II, he endured a rigorous training program to become a Navy pilot. At the time, he set a gymnastics record of 1,445 sit-ups in a 5-1/2 hour period. Part of his training included jumping off of a forty-foot platform, the exact height of the carrier deck to the water.

I throw on a tee shirt and a pair of blue jeans and pad my way across the hall into his bedroom. In short order, Mother and I get him up and settled. When his pain medication finally kicks in, Mother leaves us alone and goes downstairs to fix his breakfast.

I cross the hall again to get some old black and white pictures out of my suitcase. There are about six of them - photographs of branding cattle, a rustic cabin with mountains in the background, and a group shot of young children, including my father as a child, sitting in a flatbed wagon with his parents standing behind him.

There is nothing written on the back of these pictures and I would be a fool to pass up what might be my last opportunity to get the story behind them.

"Hey, Pop, I want to hear about your parents' trip to Wyoming."

I hand him the pictures. While he flips through each one, I rummage through my mother's bedside table for a pen and some paper.

"Well," he says, "might as well start from the beginning."

Dad told me that in 1929 when he was four years old his parents left Baltimore for a one-month trip to visit his uncle who lived in Cody, Wyoming.

"In those days, with treacherous roads and unreliable cars, it took us ten days to reach our destination. About midway through the trip, the car engine caught on fire. My father used a jug of milk to extinguish it."

"So, what did you do for food?"

"My parents solicited farmers along the way who sold them chickens and eggs."

Dad went on to tell me that when his family finally arrived in Cody, his mother was already pregnant with their third child (the one she nursed for 5 years). They had to leave their car by the river and walk 12 miles to Uncle Will's homestead.

"It took us all day," he said.

In the course of our conversation I would learn that Dad's uncle, Will Leatherman, settled in Cody in the 1920s on 320 acres (the amount allowed by the government at the time). Eventually, he built three log cabins, a barn, and a corral. To supplement his income, he guided backpacking trips through nearby Yellowstone Park. On one trip, he hoisted a bathtub on the back of a mule for a guest who also demanded that hot water be boiled for her "soak" every night. On another trip, he witnessed a horse and rider slip over the edge to their death.

Stories about Uncle Will border on the eccentric. He was a bootlegger, as well as a cattle driver, mostly traveling from Denver

This picture was taken in 1929 of Uncle Will branding cattle on his ranch in Cody, Wyoming.

to Cody. Never married, he eventually lost the ranch in a card game. On August 21, 1942, he suffered a heart attack and died.

Dad closes his eyes, my sign that he is getting tired.

"Hey, Dad, can you answer one more question?"

He opens his eyes and nods.

"Do you have any memories from that trip?"

He pauses for a moment.

"You know, I remember a pile of antlers in front of Uncle Will's cabin. When my cousin, Dick Wallace, went back to that ranch 62 years later, that pile of antlers was still there."

Just as he says that, my mother comes in with his breakfast on a tray. Her timing is perfect. While he eats, I thumb through the Wyoming pictures again. I stare at the picture with the pile of antlers in front of Uncle Will's cabin.

After Dad finishes breakfast, chaos reins and now it seems like the phone will never stop ringing. One of his neighbors drops off a dessert. Then, a social worker from hospice pays him a visit. While she and Dad are talking, my mother is preparing to leave for their condo in Bethany Beach, Delaware to take care of some business. Later in the day, my cousin comes by, telling my father that he wants to bring his wife back, but never does. It is busy around the house, just like it is when a new baby arrives, or when someone is dying.

That night, I decide to prepare Dad's favorite meal - sirloin steak cooked rare, parsley potatoes, lima beans, and salad with homemade croutons. It was a family tradition, one that we enjoyed almost every Sunday night growing up. Mother would always prepare everything but the steak, which Dad grilled to perfection on the outdoor barbeque.

I adored my father, who had a funny, playful, generous spirit. As a small child, he used to throw me up in the air and bounce me on his knee. In elementary school, it was he who helped me with my homework. And, long before I got my driver's license, Dad would let me sit next to him and steer the car with my foot on the gas pedal.

Even as a teenager, I wasn't embarrassed to be seen with my dad. In high school, he spoke to my class about the insurance business during Careers Week, a talk that was educational, yet interesting. When I started calling him by his first name, I was the envy of all my friends.

When Dad was sober, life with him was magical. But he also had a shadow side, fueled by generations of alcoholism and dysfunction. When he drank, the boundaries between he and I blurred, triggering fear and anxiety. My father was a formidable role model in my life, combining power and control with conditional love. It would take years of therapy to sort through the confusion, complexity, and conflict in our relationship.

Now, the sounds are muffled - tears amid chatter - and they are coming from my father's bedroom as I am waking up on <u>Tuesday, May 7</u>:

Dad is with Kerry, my youngest sister.

I crawl out of bed and, in my undershirt, pants, and bare feet, peek into his bedroom.

"Dad's been crying," she tells me.

My heart collapses.

"Tears of joy," he says, the corners of his mouth lifted ever so slightly. "I slept from 9:30 last night to 4:00 this morning without waking up."

"That's great, Dad," I say, feeling the heaviness in my heart lift.

"You know, it's been months since I have slept that well. A good night's rest is truly a gift."

Now, for Dad, it's the little things in life that make him happy and I am grateful for the reminder.

"How about if I get dressed, go downstairs, and make you some breakfast?" I suggest.

On the way to the kitchen, it occurs to me that I am my father's daughter. Like me, he lives to eat. For weeks, when shad were running in the spring, he ate nothing else for lunch. A thick slab of prime rib cooked medium rare needed no side dishes. Bananas and nonalcoholic beer were nirvana, that is until he started chemotherapy and lost his taste for them.

Now, constipated from the pain medication, he has no choice but to eat the bowl of fruit that I fix him instead of his usual high fat, protein breakfast of eggs and scrapple. Sitting up in bed with a wooden tray on his lap, I watch him pick through his food like a child facing a plate of vegetables. Our relationship has switched roles, for now in his vulnerable state, I have the same power and control over him as he did with me growing up.

After breakfast, while he is taking a midmorning catnap, I putter around the house doing laundry, making beds, cleaning up the kitchen, and answering the telephone. These are all things that my mother would be doing, except that she is in Delaware attending to the many details of owning a second home.

Around noon, his oldest friend stops by, armed with food from Dad's favorite restaurant in Baltimore, Chiapparelli's. The last time I went there with my father was on October 3, 1995, six days before he was diagnosed with lung cancer. It was also the day that O.J. Simpson's verdict came in. I remember everyone getting up from their tables and filing into the kitchen to watch it on television. When we heard the verdict, there was a mixed reaction among the lily-white patrons, waitresses, & owner and the mostly African American kitchen staff.

After Sam arrives with lunch from Chiapparelli's, I fall right into my pattern of taking care of the meal, just like I did in the catering business. I take the large brown bag, unwrap everything from their styrofoam containers, plate the food, and serve it.

Together, these two buddies feast on the only thing that Dad ever orders there - clams with red sauce over linguine, garlic bread, and "Chiapp's" famous tossed salad. While Sam remains focused in keeping the conversation light, I watch my father twirl, lift, and chew his food with such joy that I have to hold back my tears.

What do I owe you for lunch, Sam?" I hear Dad ask him while I clear their plates.

"Not a thing, Gordy. When I told the maitre'd it was for you, he wouldn't accept a dime."

Dad, overwhelmed with gratitude for the kindness, loses his composure and starts to cry in front of Sam. I take their plates and go downstairs to the kitchen. On my return a little while later, I walk in on Sam saying good-bye to my father. He says it as though he will see my father again, but I know that he won't. Then, without lingering, Sam descends the stairs and walks out the front door for the last time.

The day after Dad died, I flipped through his black vinyl daytimer to the last entry - Tuesday, May 7. On that day, Dad wrote: "Sam Boyer."

I look at my father. He is staring out of the window at the dogwood tree, now in full bloom.

"You look like you are ready for a nap, Dad."

"Not yet, sweetheart. I want to acknowledge my neighbor for the Boston Creme Pie and Mrs. Chiapparelli for lunch today. I'll come downstairs in a few minutes."

I brace myself knowing that he won't be able to write these two thank you notes. In the last couple of weeks, he has lost the use of his right hand and arm. Now, it is painful for me to look at his arm, and even more painful to look at his hand.

While I wait for Dad to descend the stairs, my mind becomes absorbed in another lifetime. Although my father was a successful insurance executive, his true gift was creating things with his hands. He was a master carpenter, and no room in our house went untouched by his talent. Our knotty-pine club basement was transformed into a cozy family room. He built a bathhouse in our backyard, renovated a carriage house in downtown Baltimore, and turned a run-down 1820's three-story row home into a traditional Williamsburg showplace. In 1959, he built a playhouse, which became a well-known neighborhood landmark.

The following year, *The Baltimore Sun* featured an article about the playhouse that read: "The Leatherman family, of 901 Army Road in Ruxton, have a large white house with black shutters. They also have a small white house with black shutters - a small scale reproduction of the main dwelling - located about 50 yards away. E. Gordon Leatherman built the miniature as a playhouse for his five children, who range in age from 1 to 13. He bought material from junkyards and estimates it cost about $275. Outside there is a patio, barbecue table and a breezeway connecting with a garage."

The Associated Press selected the magazine story as their "Human Interest Story of the Week." As a result, many newspapers throughout the country ran it.

Then, in 1974, Dad stopped drinking. The following year he built another, more sophisticated playhouse after the foundation on the original one rotted (to see a photograph of the second Ruxton Playhouse, see p. 230).

After my father finishes dictating the two thank you notes, I rewrite them in longhand. I will drop them in the mailbox on my way home, where I haven't been in over two days. Then, I tell my father that I am leaving.

"Do you want to see a grown man cry?" he asks me.

In my journal for <u>Wednesday, May 8</u>, I could only manage to write three words: I stayed home.

While Dad had four days left to live, I grounded myself by reconnecting with my husband, returning phone messages, opening the mail, and doing laundry.

Thursday, May 9

When the phone wakes me up around 9:00 a.m., I feel well rested. Kerry, who had spent the night with my father, is on the other end of the line.

"Dad ate a good breakfast and has read the paper, but he's still in a lot of pain," she informs me.

"How can I help?"

The original playhouse that my father built in the late 1950's.

"Bring your heating pad and get him one of those bed pillows with the padded arms so he can sit more comfortably in bed."

I tell her I won't be able to get there for a couple of hours, that I haven't even gotten in the shower yet. I also mention that on the way I want to pick up our nephew, Connor, who is the apple of Dad's eye.

"Let's surprise Dad," I tell her, adding, "it will boost his spirits."

"Great idea."

I hop in the shower, throw on some clothes, and replenish my suitcase from the day before.

By the time I fill my gas tank, pick up Connor, and buy the pillow, it is almost 3:00 p.m.

When we arrive, Dad lights up at the sight of his four-year-old grandson. The surprise turns out to be a mixed blessing. Sadly, Connor won't give my father a hug, later telling me that his hair looked too scary.

This memory is a sobering contrast from Dad's more vibrant, youthful days. My father was a strikingly handsome man with his ash blonde hair, perfect teeth, and solid physique. People were naturally drawn to his quick wit and charming personality. Around town, he was known by many people and, from the janitor in the building where he worked to the Mayor of Baltimore, everyone was on equal footing with him.

However, years of drinking, smoking, and working hard took its toll on him physically, mentally, and emotionally. In the early 1970's when the health insurance business changed - and he didn't change with it - Dad became angry and bitter. Even though he got sober and stopped smoking, he gained weight and remained out of shape for the rest of his life. Now, his hair is thinning from months of chemotherapy.

My father, E. Gordon Leatherman, in 1955.
Many people thought that
he resembled actor Van Johnson.

Dad takes the pillow with the padded arms on it while Kerry and I make him comfortable with the heating pad. Mother has returned from Delaware and is now unpacking before making dinner. While Connor hangs out in the attic playing "office", Kerry and I spend time with Dad until supper is ready. Then we help him down the stairs where he and my mother will share a meal.

His appetite, I notice, is waning with each passing day. After consuming a small portion of spaghetti, he gets up and slowly climbs the stairs to his bedroom. I note in my journal that it will be his last time on the first floor.

Throughout the week, each of my siblings is taking a night to sleep in the twin bed next to my father. I wrote: *Thursday night, I bunked with Dad. As a result of being uncomfortable, he was up a lot - back and forth from his bed to the bathroom. I, too, did not sleep well.*

Friday, May 10

Around 6:00 a.m., I wake up, walk across the hall to the guest bedroom where my mother is sleeping and ask her to take over for me. We switch beds and, for two solid hours, I sleep soundly.

The next thing I hear is the voice of my mother.

"Your father is in terrible pain again," she says, whispering through the cracked door.

I crawl out of my warm bed and into his bedroom, where I find Kerry sitting next to Dad on the love seat. Simultaneously, she is rubbing his back and sobbing.

When Dad looks up and sees me standing helplessly by the door, he says, "Your sister needs you more than I need her right now."

I rub one eye and turn to go into the bathroom.

While I am brushing my teeth, I can hear my mother on the phone with hospice. Within an hour, the social worker is there, not only soothing my father, but our frayed emotions as well.

I wrote: *The nurse gave him liquid morphine and 800 mg of Ibuprofen, refusing to leave until Dad was comfortable again.*

After she leaves, I hear Dad say to my mother, "No visitors today."

Hearing this gives me permission to go home and return the next day.

Saturday, May 11

When I arrive around 10:30 a.m., my parents' house is bustling with activity. My sister Kristan is there, having flown in from San Francisco the previous night. My brother-in-law, Nick - known as "the family rock" - was running an errand for my mother.

It is a beautiful clear day, the sky painted bright blue. My older brother Kim and his wife Gail are cleaning the patio and pulling out wrought iron furniture for the summer season. Mother is in the kitchen preparing stuffed cabbage and mashed potatoes for lunch while the grandchildren play on the grassy hill behind their brick townhouse.

I remain with Dad in his bedroom, where a heavenly breeze is pouring through the screen windows. While my younger brother Kraig gives Dad a shave, I snap a picture for my photo album. Then, he witnesses his one-year-old grandson Garrett take his first step. Around 3:00 p.m., we move him closer to the window so that he can watch the activity in the backyard.

I ask him if he wants a foot massage.

"No thanks," he answers, his voice sounding weak.

Just then, Connor comes bounding in. With as much strength as he can muster, Dad reaches out to him for a hug. Once again, Connor declines, leaving a painful memory for me to witness.

. . . .

"Am I going to die today?" my father asks me.

"I don't know, Dad."

That night, my father finishes his last meal - a quarter of a hot dog on a white roll topped with onions, mustard and pickle with a side of potato chips. While he ate, the national news was on television broadcasting the ValuJet crash in the Florida everglades.

After dinner, the numbers shrink. One by one my family leaves until there is just me, my mother, and my sister Kristan.

Sensing the end, I ask my father if he will answer a few questions about his enlistment in the Navy.

He lifts his head in slow motion and says, "I'll answer your questions if you answer mine first."

. . . .

Four months after Dad died, in a box of memorabilia, I found something that he had personally written about his enlistment:

> *Through intercession by my parents, I was granted a waiver on age; some time coming, yet was surprised and elated to be granted this waiver. Further, I was informed that should I complete pilot training, I would be the youngest Navy Pilot to serve in World War II. To this day, I must admit that I enjoy this distinction. At the very young age of 19, I had earned my coveted "Navy Wings of Gold."*

I threw it back in the box, cursing myself for waiting until the night before he died to ask him about something that obviously meant so much to him.

. . . .

By now, Dad is exhausted and it is getting late. Mother finishes brushing his teeth while Kristan, whose turn it is to "camp in" with him, administers his pain medicine. While I tuck him in, he speaks his last words to me.

"I love you," he mouths softly.

I kiss him on the forehead and go downstairs. After watching *Pretty Woman* for an hour, I am restless and go back upstairs. Kristan asks me to check on his breathing, which she says sounds strange. I agree. However, he seems comfortable, so I turn the lights out and go to bed.

A few days later, Kristan writes on the back of one of my journal pages.

> *I asked Mother to help me move Dad into a more comfortable position. We laid him out flat and covered him. Then I left the room to read my book. When I returned to get in bed, I noticed Dad's breathing was labored and noisy. He hadn't moved. For some reason, I was concerned but figured that he was okay. I slept lightly, mostly because of the noise of his breathing which were loud inhales with long, gurgling exhales. I know now that my father had already begun his transition to the other side.*

When I wake up on <u>Sunday, May 12</u>, Dad is in the same position that he was the night before. However, he still seems comfortable, so we don't disturb him. After getting dressed, Kristan and I have breakfast before taking a much-needed walk, around 10:15 a.m. When we return a couple of hours later, Mother meets us at the door.

"I think today is going to be the day. I called hospice and described his condition. They told me that he would probably go within the next three to twenty-four hours."

I go into the house and call my husband (now my "*was"band*) who is a geriatric social worker.

"Ask your mother to squeeze his hand and see if she gets a response," he says.

I get off the phone and run upstairs.

Mother squeezes his hand but there is no response. Kristan and I do the same. Again, no response. Tears flood my eyes. We call Kraig and Kerry and, by one o'clock, Dad is surrounded by everyone in his immediate family, except for Kim who said good-bye to him the day before.

My father in 1944. He always enjoyed the distinction of being the youngest pilot in World War II until he later found that President George H. W. Bush, Sr. held the title by one month.

I wrote in my journal:

For the next two hours, we sat around his bed. He opened his eyes a couple of times and gently squeezed a hand or two. Amid tears and laughter, we read to him, shared pictures, stroked him, and talked to him. At 3:10 p.m., his breathing started to change - long pauses of about 8 seconds between inhales and exhales. Then at 3:25 p.m., he took a couple short breaths, opened his eyes, looked up, took one more breath, and died.

It is Mother's Day. I am no longer aware of anyone in the room except for me and my father. This is the first time that I have witnessed someone take their last breath and, realizing he is gone, I go into mild shock.

After a while, I hear someone say, "I guess we better make the phone call."

Then I hear someone else say, "No, let's not rush this."

Dad looks so peaceful. I rub his arm and stroke his feet. When I open the lids, his hazel green eyes are crystal clear, not cloudy and yellow like they had been in the last few months.

Mother must have called hospice because the next thing I know, the social worker is quietly throwing his pain medication in a white plastic bag. I ask her to cut off some of Dad's hair for me. Before leaving, she smooths out his blanket.

I don't know who makes the call, but around 5:30 p.m., two men drive through the gate. The driver comes to the door while his assistant remains in a black van. When I hear the words "paperwork, stretcher, and crematory," it is time for me to leave. I want my last memories to be of him passing on with his loving family, not carried out by two strangers with a sheet over his body.

I take a walk. When I come back, my father's body is gone.

That night, we decide to celebrate his transition at his beloved Chiapparelli's. There are 13 of us and, when we arrive without Dad, our waitress begins to cry. She knew my father well. In his honor, we leave the chair empty at the head of the table.

Here ends my journal, but not the story.

The day after my father died, on <u>Monday, May 13, 1996</u>, a letter arrived for him in the mail.

> *Dear Mr. Leatherman, I want to take this opportunity once again to thank you for your patience and understanding when I was unable to pay my rent on time. I have had many, many landlords through the course of my lifetime and I can honestly say I have never had the respect and admiration for any of them as I have had for you. Enjoy your "retirement" and God bless you and your family!*

The following Saturday, Dad's memorial service was held in the same church where he was baptized and married. The next afternoon, on a day so hot I almost melted, the family spread some of his ashes. After dinner, my mother shared with me this story:

"A couple of months before your father was diagnosed with cancer, the power went out in the house. That's when he got up from the sofa, went into the dining room, and returned with a candle."

While Mother excused herself to go and get something, I waited in anticipation. She returned with a piece of paper in her hand and sat down.

"After lighting the candle, he told me that he had written his obituary and wanted me to see it. This is when I found out that he had already planned his memorial service."

"He really thought it through," she went on. "In fact, he had already talked to the caterer, who inadvertently asked him if he knew the date. It was also his idea to have the service on Saturday, thinking that it would help make the trip easier for his out of town friends and relatives."

Then she handed me the piece of paper. Sure enough, there in Dad's handwriting, was the plan for his memorial service.

Scanning it from top to bottom, I notice that he wrote down where to send contributions in lieu of flowers. The phone number of the caterer was on there, as was the name of the pastor. The service would start at 11:00 a.m., followed by a reception at noon. He even included directions to the church.

I was speechless, taken by my father's choice to face his own mortality so bravely. After his diagnoses in October 1995, he began to take more time off from work to be with his family. His negativity, bitterness, and anger morphed into humor, gratitude, and vulnerability. He became almost childlike, even innocent and, in the process, showed me that selflessness is really about self-love and that, in the end, love is all that matters anyway.

I handed the piece of paper back to my mother.

"No," she said, "you keep it."

"Because?"

"Because I know that you will be the one to keep his memory alive."

Eventually, I did a photo album about his life. With a camera strapped over my shoulder, I interviewed his family and friends, visited his favorite haunts, and poured through mounds of pictures, papers and memorabilia. The project consumed hundreds of hours and took me four months to finish.

On the last album page, underneath a picture of his grandson Connor - the one who wouldn't hug him - I wrote the following story.

"Four years after my father died, Mother was going through a steamer trunk in the attic. In it, she found a white envelope with the word 'Popa' written on it. Inside, there was a note from Connor:

*Dear popa I love you atot when you
died I was very sat but I will never forget
you, CL.*

In those last final days of my father's life, Connor didn't want to hug "Popa" because his hair looked too scary. After Dad died, on one of his visits to see my mother, Connor quietly went to the attic, wrote that note, and then buried it in bottom of the trunk. Clearly, he found his own, unique way to say good-bye to my father.

Family faces are magic mirrors.
Looking at people who belong to us,
we see the past, present, and future.

– Gail Lumet Buckley

I did not lose myself all at once.
I rubbed out my face over the years washing my pain,
the same way carvings on stone are worn down by water.

– Amy Tan

LAYERS OF CLUTTER

I don't know about you, but I thrive on the warm fuzzy feeling of order in my life. Loose ends and I have rarely been a good match, especially when it comes to my home environment. But, even beyond my living *s p a c e*, life is a study in layers; there is always a higher plateau, a deeper emotion, another challenge to tackle...

...which brings me to the subject of our possessions.

The top, or surface, layer will help to loosen you up. So, go ahead and toss out those mystery keys, anything that is broken and can't be fixed, old newspapers, bank statements from twenty years ago, dead batteries, moldy food, and puzzles with missing pieces.

Next, the middle layer which is about releasing things like clothes that haven't been worn in the last year, downsizing quantities, and giving away things that you clearly don't want, like, or have outgrown. You may decide to recycle or give away ten things a day. To increase your chances of success, always break it down and stay focused. Getting ahead of yourself and thinking about all that has to be done will cause you to give up.

Then there is the most challenging of all, the bottom layer. This is when it feels like therapy, where we come face to face with our fears. These are the possessions that belong(ed) to a family member, friend, or significant other and usually are connected to a specific memory or emotion. Usually, they are things that have become a burden to take care of, take up too much *s p a c e*, or leave you feeling guilty at the thought of passing them on.

The following ideas are geared toward targeting the bottom layer:

1. Loan things out with the condition that the item be returned to you if that person no longer wants or needs it. For example, "give" your childhood rocking chair to a niece, nephew, or godchild. Similarly, offer furniture to family and friends so that you can "visit" the object.

2. To keep a tangible, visual memory of an object "alive," take photographs of things that you don't want to keep anymore. Or, have someone record you holding the possession while you talk about it.

3. To preserve memories, make a collage, patchwork quilt, or wall hanging using squares from old fabrics, uniforms, blankets, and childhood clothing. Attach campaign buttons, patches, metals, awards ribbons, etc. Make a small pillow out of the fabric from your wedding dress.

4. If you are a collector, keep only your favorite representative samples and photograph the rest to display in a photo album.

5. Old pictures, papers, and magazine articles can be scanned onto a computer disk. Now that you can access almost anything on the Internet, let go of those old college texts and heavy reference books.

6. Store things that you don't want in a box without labeling the contents. Then close it up, date it, and store it away. After one year, see if you can give the box away without opening it. If not, ask yourself, "If I didn't need or miss anything, what would make me want to keep it now?"

***The objects that we keep
become our past frozen in solid form.***

– Sandra Felton
Messes Anonymous

**At the beginning of the school year,
the teacher gave his students one rule:**

"If you make a problem, I'll do something."

*(To increase your potential for power,
refrain from disclosing the consequences.)*

LIFE WITH KIDS

Just for the record, I am not a mother - at least biologically speaking. For five years, I was a "big sister" to a less fortunate inner city kid. I am also a village person, an aunt, and a godparent. And, in the world according to my Norwich terrier, Sweet Potato, I am the mommy of her universe.

Children come and go in my life, but they remain among my greatest teachers since they model what I most need to learn - living in the present moment. They also lack any sense of time and, some days, I wish I did too.

For better or worse, children will inherit our gene pool, absorb our laundry list of clutter, and may even adopt a similar lifestyle. They will imbibe our fears, feelings, beliefs, and attitudes. And their view of themselves and the world is reflected back to them through us, just like it was when we were young and impressionable.

As an adult, I am responsible for my actions and behavior. For example, some of my old beliefs have been triggered by children. One is that in order for them to love me, I have *to do* something. I believed that *to be* who I am is not enough, so I would overindulge them, often with negative consequences. So, in order to affect a different outcome, I had to source the root cause of the problem. What I realized is that it stems from my being loved conditionally, not just in my own family but from teachers, peers, and society.

When you experience a trigger reaction, sometimes it's easier to scapegoat your children than it is to clean up your side of the street. Kids are needy by nature, so if you find that their neediness makes you angry and resentful, chances are you didn't get your needs met as a child. As a parent, it's your responsibility to decide what you are going to do about the problem, not what you are going to make your child do about it. To keep this fresh in your mind, write the following note and tape it on your bathroom mirror:

"I am looking at the problem.
Therefore, I am responsible for the solution."

In closing, I would like to say that I couldn't have written this chapter without my sister, Kristan.* As a nationally sought-after parenting coach, family life consultant, and workshop facilitator for teachers and parents, she comes equipped with immeasurable amounts of common sense, creative ideas on how to elicit cooperation, and a natural ability to support parents in communicating effectively with their children. Many of her ideas, reminders, and tips will create more *s p a c e* in your life.

1. The root cause of most relationship problems is inadequate communication systems, i.e., actions, things, information, and ideas that interact effectively with others. One example is if your preschooler needs your attention while you are on the phone, ask him or her to tap your shoulder instead of tolerating verbal interruptions. With good systems, your children will know what is expected of them. Then change the system as your child's developmental needs change - a great stress reducer for you.

2. Since structure gives children a sense of security, set firm, yet fair, boundaries and rules. By disciplining with consistency, you become predictable and they will feel safe. You will gain their trust and respect if you adopt a long-term point of view.

3. Strive to give your kids a conditional yes instead of saying no all the time. Here are three examples.

a. Your child wants a cookie. "Yes, after dinner."

b. Your child wants pierced ears. "Yes, when you turn thirteen."

c. The child wants to play on the computer. "Yes, once you have finished your homework," or "Yes, after you have cleaned up your room."

4. Children will develop self-esteem on their own if they are held accountable for their behavior. Therefore, avoid jumping in to protect or rescue them. Natural consequences teach them how to handle frustration and hardship, a reality that they will have to face in the outside world.

5. The average child has 15% to 25% less free time than their parents due, in part, to the amount of homework which has tripled since 1981. To maintain balance, allow them freedom within structure. Since most kids have homework, the structure is that they have to do it. The freedom might be that they can do it before or after dinner.

6. Children will obey you out of respect or fear. Spanking is an easy, effective, short-term tactic that works because it stops the behavior. So does verbal abuse, including threats, ultimatums, and assumptions. Kids who are disciplined in this way will build up feelings of resentment and anger. Lying, avoidance, and wanting to retaliate can follow. Parenting children without physical or verbal muscle requires more time, patience, and creativity. If you are reasonable, show encouragement, and offer an explanation, you will gain their cooperation. Confront the misbehavior and give them consequences that you will enforce.

7. Avoid asking "why" questions. Children can feel shamed if they don't know why or if they don't have the "right" answer. Instead ask, "What is your understanding of this situation?" or "What were you trying to accomplish when you did that?" If you ask differently, they may respond differently.

8. It is usually more effective to give kids less information than to give them too much and have them hear things that they wished they hadn't. If they want more, they will ask. If your five year old asks where babies came from, say, "From Mommy's tummy." Then wait for the next question, which is your cue that they want more information.

9. When it comes to offering choices to your kids, less is more. For example, you might say, "You can clean up your room now or in 10 minutes." If they say, "I'll do it in 10 minutes," then set a timer. Whenever you need to set boundaries around time, ask them to listen for the bell on the timer. That way, the timer becomes the center of attention, not you. This also teaches them to be accountable for what they said they would do.

10. Sibling rivalry is an effective attention grabber, so once you intervene, the focus shifts to you. Encourage them to resolve their own conflict. Then ask them how they did it. This encourages children to solve their own problems and teaches them conflict resolution.

11. Teach your child responsibility by establishing regular chores. With your guidance, even a two year old can help carry his or her dirty clothes to the laundry room. Give them choices and let them help you draw up a chart that gets posted. Again, link consequences to the misbehavior. If they don't integrate the habit of helping out early on, then you will be doing all the work down the road. This practice will also create less struggle later on.

12. Put together a visual chart with magazine pictures of children putting on clothes, brushing their teeth, eating breakfast, etc. You could even take photographs of your child doing it. This is a valuable tool around their routine time. If they forget what to do, tell them to check their chart. The chart becomes the guide, not you.

13. Independence teaches self-reliance, so back off from giving your kids too much assistance, a counterproductive

measure. The more you allow them to do, the more capable they will feel.

14. Schedule quiet time - to reflect, rest, and renew. Create a small *s p a c e* in their room to be alone. There, they might store a favorite toy, blanket, music, and/or book. Involve them in the process of putting their *s p a c e* together. It will peak their interest and reduce the struggle when you ask them to spend time in their "special" place.

15. Teach your children good organizational habits. At least once a year, go through their closets and toys, doing it with them, not for them. That way, they can be a part of the decision-making process when it comes to what they want to keep, give away, or toss. Take them with you to the donation center. Explain the "one in, one out guideline" - i.e., when they buy something, they must let go of something else. Make a game out of it.

16. Start a new holiday tradition. Buy one or two special gifts for your child. You may find that what your holiday lacks in commercialism will more than make up for with peace of mind. So that the expectation is clear, tell them how many presents they are going to receive. Quality gifts are stimulating, fun, and send a positive message.

17. Set aside one trunk, box, or storage bin for each child and begin to gather memorabilia for them - swatches of fabric from clothes that they wore, a lock of hair, school report cards, photographs, art projects, diplomas, and certificates. To avoid overload, have your children choose two or three of their favorite art projects at the end of the school year, and discard the rest.

18. One of the greatest gifts that you can instill in your children is good eating habits. To get them involved, allow them to be a part of the menu planning. Take them grocery shopping and let them help you choose the produce. For age appropriate kids, read labels together. Talk to them about the difference between processed and whole foods. The more you involve them,

the more they will participate. And that will help you in the long run, especially if you teach them how to cook. Jessica Seinfeld's book, *Deceptively Delicious*, will give you creative ideas on how to sneak healthier food into their diet with recipes such as yellow squash in macaroni and cheese, spinach in brownies, and sweet potato in pancakes.

19. When you transition from processed foods, remind your children that eating healthier doesn't mean that they have to give up their favorite foods. It's just that now their favorite foods are treats. Treats give them something to look forward to, and it gives you more bargaining power.

20. Young children are the best regulators of their own food. They know what their body needs and how much. Over-managing them hinders their ability to develop self-control and to trust the natural rhythm of their body.

21. For age appropriate children, store healthy snacks on lower shelves. This teaches them independence and removes some of the responsibility from you.

22. Talk with them about the power of food and how it can affect the way that they think, behave, and feel. Point out consequences, such as stomach aches, headaches, and fatigue. Explain to them that their body is like a car (or whatever object they can identify with) that requires good fuel, proper maintenance, and regular care in order to run well.

23. On Halloween, instead of candy, give out stickers, glow bracelets or necklaces, and bubble wands. To reduce power struggles over the ubiquitous amount of candy that your kids bring home, offer choices around how much your kids get to keep and how much they get to eat. For example, you might allow them to keep half of the amount they bring home. Then, offer them the choice of having one or two pieces per day.

24. Kids don't miss what they have never tasted. From the beginning, it's best to give them water rather than juice and

sodas, which set up sugar cravings. If you've already started, wean them by adding water to the soda or juice.

25. For the immune system, the best offense is a good defense. Strive to give your children a well balanced diet and keep their stress levels to a minimum. Sick children will not simplify your life. Choose a pediatrician who works with the body's natural ability to heal itself. Antibiotics work for ear infections, sinus infections, and strep throat. They don't work for viral infections, such as colds and mild coughs.

26. If your child wants a pet, give him or her a stuffed animal to feed, walk, and play with for one week. If s/he doesn't want to get up early in the morning to go outside and walk the "dog," then that is your sign that they probably aren't ready to help you with the responsibility.

27. Avoid revolving your life around your children; they aren't going to be the center of attention in the real world. Having to adjust outside of the home will be difficult enough, especially when they go to school.

28. Encourage and guide them to develop their intuition by first asking and then listening for the answer from within. Keep it light and make it fun for them. This will give them the confidence to trust their choices later on in life without having to seek out the opinion of others.

29. Begin to weave gratitude into their lives by telling them what you are grateful for. Before they go to bed, point out the blessings with every challenge, disappointment, or hurt.

30. Let the spirit of who they are be your guide. Encourage their interests and abilities. Give them *s p a c e* to be creative. Children who are guided with love, respect, and understanding grow up to be happy, well adjusted adults.

*For more information about Kristan Leatherman, M.S. and her work with parents, children and educators, go to her website at: RaisingMillionaireBabies. com. Her book, *Millionaire Babies or Bankrupt Brats? Love and Logic Solutions to Teaching Kids About Money* focuses on how to raise self-reliant children in a self-indulgent world. Chapters include how to teach personal and fiscal responsibility by providing kids experiences around learning how to spend, save, earn, borrow, invest and share money wisely.

You can learn many things from kids.
How much patience you have, for example.

– Franklin P. Jones

Living with integrity means: Not settling for less than what you know you deserve in your relationships. Asking for what you want and need from others. Speaking your truth, even though it might create conflict or tension. Behaving in ways that are in harmony with your personal values. Making choices based on what you believe, and not what others believe.

– Barbara DeAngelis

LIVING WITH INTEGRITY

Obviously, I am a simplicity aficionado. For thirty years, since the early 1970s, I have explored just about every crevice in my life, redefined the word clutter, and done a fair amount of letting go. I choose to do this because living with *s p a c e* is the elixir that nourishes my soul.

Integrity is one word that we don't always associate with *s p a c e*. Webster defines integrity as "adherence to moral and ethical principles; soundness of moral character; honesty." To be rigorously honest, to practice loving kindness towards myself and others, and to live consciously actually creates *s p a c e* and opens up the flow of energy. Lack of integrity does just the opposite by reversing the energy, closing doors, and shutting down opportunities.

I don't know about you, but I believe in karma. For example, if a cashier has given me too much money and I take it anyway, then somewhere, sometime, someone is going to cheat me. It may not come back to me in the same way, but it will come back to me. Maybe it will show up in the form of being betrayed.

It is an illusion to think that being a good person is enough to allow us even the smallest deception. After all, no one will know but us, but it doesn't work that way. Karma means that you don't get away with anything. Karma is the universal law that says "what goes around, comes around." It is not meant to punish us. It is meant to keep reminding us to live with integrity.

Here are eight ways to live with integrity:

1. *KEEP YOUR WORD.* If you say you are going to do something, then do it. If you can't live up to your word, communicate that. Honoring your word also makes you dependable.

2. *BE HONEST.* Authenticity is a form of honesty. The more authentic you are, the more authentic others will be towards you. Agreeing with people when you don't, or saying yes when you mean no is a form of dishonesty. Tell the truth, to yourself as well as others. William Shakespeare says, "No legacy is so rich as honesty."

3. *TAKE CARE OF YOURSELF.* Strive to maintain a healthy body, mind, and spirit. Integrity is about loving yourself so that you can live your life to the fullest. Surround yourself with supportive people who are also committed to doing the same.

4. *BUY PRODUCTS AND SERVICES THAT ARE BACKED WITH INTEGRITY.* Spend your money on businesses that care about people, sell environmentally friendly products, or who donate a portion of their profits for the betterment of the world. As much as your budget allows, support organic farmers. Consume meat and eggs from companies whose treatment toward animals is not only humane but who raise them without pesticides, hormones, and drugs. Choose to eat "live," whole natural foods over foods that are stripped of their nutrients.

5. *PRACTICE THE FOUR "Rs."* *RESPECT* other peoples' time. *RETURN* phone calls and e-mails in a timely manner. *RESPOND* to invitations. Be *RESPONSIBLE* for your actions and behavior.

6. *BE TRUSTWORTHY.* When someone asks for your confidence, honor their request.

7. _RESOLVE CONFLICT WITH COMPASSION,_
KINDNESS, AND UNDERSTANDING. Put the same energy that
you would use to talk about the problem into finding a solution.
Use "I" statements when resolving conflict. It's not so much the
nature of the conflict as how you handle yourself while you're
going through it. If someone has wronged you, download your
feelings and then turn it over to karma.

8. _LIVE CONSCIOUSLY._ The roots of conscious living
are grounded in our desire to change and grow. It is in the
present moment that we are truly alive, aware of who we are, and
able to make choices that effect a positive difference, not only for
ourselves, but in the lives of those we touch.

**Integrity is telling myself the truth.**
**Honesty is telling the truth to other people.**

– Spencer Johnson

Neither a lofty degree of intelligence nor imagination nor both together go to the making of genius. Love, love, love, that is the soul of genius.

— Mozart

MARNIE

Unconditional love. You only need one person to love you unconditionally, and if your childhood was difficult, one will be enough. Marnie was my bona fide earth angel for forty-one years and, in spite of my mischievous behavior which included testing her ability to love me unconditionally, she remained steadfast.

Marnie was my maternal grandmother. I adored her because she gave me the s p a c e to be who I was. She was also a Scorpio, and I've never met a Scorpio I didn't like. We would have been born on the same day had I come into the world 8 hours and 34 minutes earlier. Still, we always celebrated our birthdays as if they were one.

Every summer, my sister Kristan and I would spend a week with my grandparents. There, I was the center of her world. Marnie would fix me eggs for breakfast using only the whites because she knew that I didn't like the yolks. I preferred bread crusts, so she would cut them off, butter them, and roll them into neat little spirals. Of course, she didn't like egg yolks or the center of the bread either, but she would sacrifice them for me.

Behind their country house was a pasture, as far as the eye could see, where a large herd of ponies in every color and size grazed in leisure. Across the road was the Miller's dairy farm where Marnie would buy her weekly supply of eggs and milk. She got her honey from Mrs. Bea, her next door neighbor, who also kept a flock of sheep. Today, the sheep and cows and ponies are gone and the fields are now a landscape of concrete with new homes, condominiums, and traffic lights.

Marnie was an old soul, a wonderful listener, and a gifted teacher. I learned how to sew and make crafts and paint with her guidance. At night, in a canvas hammock just off of the kitchen porch, my sister and I would crawl in with her to stargaze, sing, and listen to stories about her girlhood. When my occasional bouts of "bratism" surfaced, her method of discipline was gentle, yet effective. "Someone isn't acting very nice," she would say.

Born in 1901, Marnie was raised with four brothers - two older and two younger. Her father worked for the railroad while her mother stayed home and tended to her family. My great grandmother was a very religious woman who didn't allow dancing, playing cards, or work of any kind on Sunday. For this clan, it was a day of devotion to the Lord.

Marnie was religious too, but she never talked about it unless you asked. I liked that about her. She never told anyone what to do, nor did she dispense unsolicited advice. Of course, it was this very characteristic that made her the perfect person to seek out in times of trouble.

Even so, she had the ability to make the best of what seemed like a disappointing life. Her favorite brother was killed in an explosion while attending Lehigh University. Her mother-in-law treated her with disdain. My grandfather served in the Army during World War I, where his job was to rescue injured soldiers and remove dead bodies from the battlefields. The war would take its toll on their marriage after he returned home nervous, impatient, and controlling.

To cope, Marnie raised two daughters and stayed busy. In the summer, she tended her vegetable garden - a carpet of sunshine and love - and canned her life-giving foods. Throughout the fall and winter months, she painted in oils, made clothes from designer patterns, played the piano, created museum-quality miniature rooms, and refinished furniture. By spring, her house was ready to be aired out and cleaned from top to bottom. That's

Marnie holding my two year old mother, 1925. It won a photography contest and was later featured in a magazine. Marnie told me that the photographer had to bribe my mother to hug her.

when the Popsicle sticks would surface to remove dirt from the corners of the windows.

"I will never live long enough to accomplish everything that I want to do," she would often tell me.

For Marnie, "grandmotherhood" was more fulfilling than being a mother. She went to great lengths to make her six grandchildren feel extra special - handmade Halloween costumes, Valentine's Day cards with money in them, and Easter baskets. One year, for Christmas, she made us a collection of puppets to go along with a little stage that my grandfather built.

After my ailing grandfather was moved to a nursing home, Marnie downsized to a smaller apartment, sloughed off a lot of weight, and lived quietly with her many possessions. Even in her nineties, she continued to clip interesting articles from magazines and newspapers in an effort to keep her mind active. She would much rather discuss ideas - what was happening in the world and what I was doing in my life - than gossip.

She wouldn't give in to old age either, saying, "I'm not ready to die yet." But, on Super Bowl Sunday, January 31, 1993, at the age of 92, she died of congestive heart failure. I remember during half-time that Michael Jackson sang "We are the World." The day before, I witnessed the birth of my goddaughter Hannah - a confluence of miracle and loss. It was thrilling and exhausting and, by the end of the day, all I wanted to do was go home.

My intuition was urging me to go and see Marnie on my way home from the birthing center, but I couldn't muster up the energy. Sadly, this decision came with a price. The next morning, with only my parents at her side, she made her transition.

. . . .

In my late twenties, I had the opportunity to pass on what Marnie had given me. Joe was three years old when I met him, the fourth of five children born into a welfare family. At the age of two, he was taken from his mother and father to live in a foster home. Two years later, when Joe was five, he returned home to live with his parents. That's when we met, through my father.

For the next three years, I was Joe's magical person. Every week, we hung out and did fun stuff together. He brought out the little kid in me and I restored his faith in humanity. Sadly, we lost touch when he was sent away to live with an aunt, and later to an out-of-state foster home. For a troubled child, it only takes the unconditional love of one person to prevent him or her from falling through the cracks.

. . . .

A few years after Marnie died, I went to see a psychic, who told me that her spirit had just come into the room.

"She is so beautiful and bursting with love!" the woman exclaimed. "She's also carrying an armload of dolls."

Chills trickled down my spine.

This woman had no way of knowing that Marnie's dolls were her most prized possession.

What lies behind us and what lies before us
are tiny matters compared to what lies within us.

— Oliver Wendell Holmes

It's the s p a c e s in life that I like the most.

– Jerry Seinfeld

MORE ABOUT S P A C E

I f *s p a c e* were a person, she would be my best friend. I love *s p a c e* and, most days, I am happy when there's an abundance of it on my calendar. I also need a *s p a c e* to call my own and I enjoy *s p a c e* in my relationships. I do yoga to create *s p a c e* in my body and, in meditation, I practice expanding the *s p a c e s* between the thoughts in order to experience my true nature.

But, there's another kind of *s p a c e*, a more frightening kind, one that for many years was among my biggest fears. When I began my quest to become more conscious, I knew I would need to make peace with it. Because, when the going gets tough, being comfortable in *s p a c e* was at the heart of my personal recovery.

Healing our past doesn't necessarily require an archeological dig. Very often, opportunities are no further than our next breath. I call them reactive experiences, where something gets triggered because it feels like a similar dynamic from a previous, pivotal experience.

Once I figured this out, I began to pay attention to anything that evoked a strong reaction or brought up strong feelings such as sadness, anger, or hurt. This could stem from the sound of a person's voice, the way they said something, what they said or the inflection in their voice. They might look or smell like someone who hurt you or they may do something that activates a painful memory but, whatever it is, see it as a blessing.

Years ago, a friend of mine flew in from Colorado for a Grateful Dead concert. After the show, Dan crashed at my place. The next morning, while I was still sleeping, he left without saying good-bye. When I woke up to an empty apartment, I started sobbing uncontrollably in primal, guttural tones. The pain was so deep that I called a friend for support.

Days later, I was able to source this trigger reaction to a childhood memory of having fallen out of my bed in the middle of the night. It wasn't the crash that made the experience traumatic, but a haunting, forbidding sound of a woman's voice coming from the impenetrably wooded area behind our house.

It happened in slow motion, the frightful sound beginning to filter through the window into the cool, dark stillness of my bedroom. The sound grew louder, more intense, and eerie. In an attempt to protect myself, I started to scream for my mother. When she didn't hear me, I put my hands over my ears and curled up in a fetal position. Just when I was sure that this mystery woman would thrust herself at me, everything fell into a pool of silence.

I couldn't move.

The only sound was my breathing - hard and rugged. I opened my eyes and looked up at the ceiling in my bedroom. Then I closed them and waited for my mother. Realizing that there was no rescue in sight, I pulled myself up off of the floor, got back in bed, and buried the trauma.

I had experienced what it was like to be in s p a c e - without a safety net - where the seeds of abandonment took root, along with not knowing, having to wait, and feeling vulnerable. When Dan left my apartment that morning without saying good-bye, it triggered in me some of those same dynamics from that first "screen" memory of feeling abandoned by my mother.

I continued to attract experiences that could be traced back to subsequent, earlier traumas. One involved a love affair with a man who was like my father - good looking and successful - but also alcohol dependent. It wasn't long before his charm gave way to mental and emotional abuse. Ultimately, the guy shifted his affection to another woman, just like my father did when my sister was born.

Early childhood traumas are undeniably impressionable. As infants, we don't separate ourselves from our mothers. When our needs don't get met - whether it's getting our diaper changed, being fed when we are hungry, or being held if we are crying - it feels like something is missing in us, that somehow we are flawed. As a result, we spend the rest of our lives trying to fill that hole inside.

Growing up, I was so afraid of *s p a c e* that I used food, sleep, shopping, nicotine, alcohol, and marijuana to fill it up. For years, living with issues in my tissues, I know well the consequences that come with avoiding *s p a c e.* One of my side effects was digestive problems because I couldn't "digest" what was happening to me. The body is like nature in one very specific way; it will tolerate a lot of abuse before it retaliates.

After I got sober and began my recovery process, I discovered a technique called *feeling into the core.* It's a wonderful way to practice becoming more comfortable in *s p a c e.* Since our issues are an energetic problem and have very little to do with the intellect, recovery is much faster than talk therapy.

To begin, get comfortable with your eyes closed, become quiet, and allow the memory to surface. Now, notice where you feel it in your body. It may show up as a knot in your stomach, an ache in your heart, tightness in the throat, or an overall heaviness in the body.

Once you connect the feeling to the memory, begin to breathe into the center of the sensation. This will help bring you back to the place where the memory was first created. Take as much time as you need for this and use an affirmation if it helps. Be in your inner *s p a c e* until there is nothing left but a sense of peace and calm. You may find that although it can be a cathartic experience, it doesn't have to be for healing to occur. Let go of the outcome and allow the experience to happen just as it's supposed to.

Even though I've done a lot of inner work, the scars will remain. It will never be easy for me to give up control, be patient, and feel vulnerable. Because of my abandonment issues, I will always be sensitive in situations where it feels like people, places, and situations are "pulling away" from me.

Today, I know intellectually that my mother may have been out and left me with a babysitter, or didn't hear me crying that night many years ago. Yet, it's still my responsibility to heal my past so that I won't recreate the same destructive patterns in my adult life.

*An addiction is anything we do to avoid hearing
the messages that body and soul are trying to send us.*

– Marion Woodman

People who take risks
generally make about two big mistakes a year.
People who don't take risks
generally make about two big mistakes a year.

– Peter F. Drucker

MUTE

"**S**o, what would you say if I decided to become a voluntary mute?"

I opened the car window to breathe in the earthy, back-to-school smell of autumn. It was a glorious midweek September morning as Terry and I flew past the last exit on the Merritt Parkway heading south towards New York City.

School was back in session, creating more *s p a c e*, less traffic, and a happier me to be around. After a two-week vacation basking in the tranquility and beauty of Cape Cod, my mind felt refreshed, my body and soul restored. The Merritt Parkway is halfway between The Cape and our home in Maryland.

I love The Merritt with its hairpin exits, grass shoulders, and tiny, stone facade gas stations. Except for the late model cars, it is a drive back through time. Clearly this road, built in the 1930's, is in a class by itself. Each bridge overpass was designed by a different architect. The four lanes, divided by a small, metal guard rail, wind their way through some of the most expensive real estate in the country.

Over the years, The Merritt hasn't changed much, which also makes it dangerous to drive at high speeds. However, with the State of Connecticut's effort to make it safer - like widening the exits - it loses some of its charm and appeal.

"So, what would you think about me being a mute?" I asked Terry again.

He smiled. By now, we had been married ten years and nothing surprised him about me.

"Where on earth did you come up with the idea of becoming a voluntary mute?"

I reached in the back of the car for the cooler and pulled out some roasted cashews, a bottle of water, and a small cluster of seedless black grapes.

"Want some?" I asked, plucking a few grapes from their sturdy vine.

"Maybe later."

After washing down the fruit and nuts with a swig of cold water, I told him about this teacher who shared with the class that her father decided to become a voluntary mute.

"She told us that he would walk around in an old, tattered bathrobe that looked like dreadlocks and scribble notes on a pad of paper."

"Go on," Terry said with mild interest.

"Apparently, he didn't talk to anyone for six months. Even though her friends knew that he was a little strange, she was embarrassed to bring them around when he was home."

I opened the glove compartment and pulled out some paper and a pen. So far, we were making good time as we approached the Tappan Zee Bridge. Once we cleared the tollbooth, I looked to the left for the Manhattan skyline. There it was, way out yonder, suspended somewhere between the Hudson and Heaven.

"Ever since she told me that story about her father, I can't get it out of my mind."

"I can relate to that," he said, now fidgeting with the buttons on his cell phone.

I looked over at this kind, supportive man with beautiful strawberry blonde hair, freckles, and wire rim glasses. Clearly, he loves me for my quirky behavior and quasi liberalism and quest for truth. On a domestic note, he can pack a dishwasher better than anyone I've ever seen.

We moved without incident through moderate post rush hour traffic toward New Jersey's Garden State Parkway. Our two dogs, Sweet Potato and Kiwi, were sound asleep in the back seat, one big furry pile of unconditional love.

The Garden State Parkway is everything that The Merritt isn't - eight lanes, tract homes, billboards, and buildings devoid of character. As we approached the first of four 35 cent toll plazas, I told Terry that I wasn't going to talk anymore until we got home.

Again, he smiled, but for a very different reason.

He knew that I couldn't tell him how to drive or what toll lane to avoid or when to slow down. One time, at home, when I was trying to control him, he grabbed the television remote, pointed it towards me, and hit the mute button.

From the passenger side pocket, I pulled out a magazine to use underneath my lined 6" x 9" writing pad and wrote my first note: *Mutes are great listeners. Talk away.*

Then I shoved the pad in front of him to read. When he didn't say anything for a few minutes, I preoccupied my mind with what to write next. We wove our way through the traffic and the toll plazas on the Garden State with our E-Z pass, the best invention, in my opinion, since the debit card.

Finally, I thought of something and wrote: *Thanks for packing the car this morning.*

"You're welcome," he said.

When it comes to travel, Terry is definitely a take-charge person, or is it his penchant for needing to control? No matter. I am happy that he is more than willing to make all of the arrangements. At the airport, while he handles our luggage and checks to see if our frequent flyer miles are accounted for, I practice yoga in an abandoned gate area. On road trips, he shleps our suitcases, technology equipment, and dog paraphernalia to the car and packs it with precision. Even on the water, I look like the well-tended wife perched on the white, padded chair as he captains our motorboat, NAMASTE.

Again, I picked up my pen and wrote: *Are you still enjoying the Leads group?*

"Ahhhhhh.....yeah," he answered, now distracting himself with the radio dial.

I forgot that this is a predictable answer to a closed ended question. Closed ended questions usually elicit a one word response such as yes, no, fine, maybe, okay, etc. But, if I remember to ask open ended questions, my chances of getting more information are almost always guaranteed.

I made a second attempt and wrote: Bring me up to date on the Leads Club.

"Actually, Berlin showed up a couple of weeks ago. All of her hard work is finally paying off. She picked up two new clients."

Better answer, I thought.

By now, we were through the fourth toll plaza on The Garden State Parkway bound for The New Jersey Turnpike, a.k.a. Interstate 95. The car clock read 1:00 p.m. We were still making great time.

Interstate 95 is the fastest, most direct route from Maine to Florida. However, even on a good day it still has lousy rest stop food, smog, and endless road repair projects. Bad days include backups, made more unbearable if one desperately needs to use the bathroom or is dealing with a carload of needy kids. And, let's not forget the near-death experiences, like moving through a rainstorm sandwiched between two tractor-trailers.

Of course, we could travel a longer, more scenic route through quaint little towns with family-owned restaurants and historic points of interest, but we never do. The destination seems to be the focus - as if my life depended on it - instead of enjoying the process of getting there. And you can bet that if I am choosing this on the road, than I am also doing it in other areas of my life, too.

Once we made it through the automated tollbooth to pick up our ticket on the New Jersey Turnpike, I wrote in caps: *LET'S STOP.*

Terry nodded.

With ten miles to go before the next rest area, I thought about the amount of verbal clutter that filters through our lives every day. Small talk can be a real energy drain, no doubt the very reason that I don't care for the ultimate verbal workout - cocktail parties.

Finally, we pulled into The Joyce Kilmer Rest Area. Fourteen years before, on my way to Woodstock, New York for a family wedding, I stopped there to stretch my legs and use the bathroom. I asked an employee in the snack shop if he knew who Joyce Kilmer was. It turns out that Joyce Kilmer was a *he* from New Jersey who had written the sentimental poem, *Trees*, nearly a century ago.

Now, after leaving the bathroom, I went into that same snack shop looking for a carton of milk. There wasn't any in the refrigerator, so I whipped out my paper and pen and wrote: *Do you have any 1% milk?*

I walked over to the service counter and held up the piece of paper. The man looked at what I had written. Then he looked at me. Then he looked at the piece of paper again and came out from behind the counter. He couldn't have been nicer, proceeding to look in the refrigerator. Then, he went in the back, leaving several people standing in line behind me.

A few minutes later, he returned empty-handed. "I'm terribly sorry," he said, "but we must be out of it."

I soaked up the star treatment, thanked him, and left thinking that being a mute had some pretty grand advantages.

After Terry filled our gas tank and I walked Sweet Potato and Kiwi in the designated pet area, we drove back into the cement jungle of what is known as "The Peanut State."

Again, I reached in the back seat for the cooler. The mere thought of food usually primes my appetite, even when I'm not hungry. In it were two, large whole wheat tortillas stuffed with homemade tuna salad, lettuce, and slices of sweet Vidalia onion. To satisfy my craving for crunchy food, I brought some grape tomatoes and celery, carrot, and jicama sticks.

In lieu of writing, I waved my hand in Terry's direction and pointed to the wrap.

"Sure," Terry said, opening it with both hands, his left knee pressed against the steering wheel. I set the bag of veggies on the console between our seats, swallowed two digestive enzyme capsules, and wolfed down my lunch.

After Terry finished his wrap, he asked me if I had anything sweet.

I shook my head. With no dessert on hand, he gave me a familiar look of resignation before taking another sip through the straw of a large Diet Coke that he purchased at The Joyce Kilmer Rest Area.

I opened my cassette box and pulled out a homemade tape with a mix of female singers and songwriters - Joni Mitchell, Kate Bush, Julia Fordham, and Nancy Griffith. While Nancy Griffith sang *Lone Star,* I began to contemplate this crazy idea of becoming a voluntary mute.

If I chose to do it, even for a week, there would need to be some planning. First of all, I wouldn't be able to answer the phone. If my dogs ran off, I couldn't call them when we were out walking. I would have to cancel my yoga classes, or find a substitute. My Tuesday lunch class would understand; they have been with me for a long time. Together, we could do silent sun salutations. However, my Thursday night class would think I had gone over the edge and never come back.

Just then, red taillights sprouted everywhere and the traffic slowed on the turnpike. This makes me anxious, especially when I can't see what's up ahead. So I did the only thing that I could control and continued to plan my attempt to become a voluntary mute.

I thought about going to the grocery store, or anywhere for that matter. I would have to carry a pen and paper - which wasn't a big deal - but what if I ran into someone who knew me. To cover my tracks, I could always write *laryngitis* or *sore throat - hurts to talk.*

I know that my excuses are a sign of resistance, which never holds the s p a c e for me to take a risk.

My mind grew restless from the traffic backup. I shifted from one sit bone to the other and stretched through each leg. At least the traffic was moving, even if the car was only in first gear.

More than once, due to a serious accident, I have seen the turnpike completely shut down, forcing the police to funnel everyone down to one single exit. For miles, we zoom past thousands and thousands of cars sitting idle on the other side of the guard rail. And, in every one of those cars, someone is wanting something - a bathroom break, a drink, some comfort food, to be anywhere but stuck on Interstate 95 in New Jersey.

I returned to my fantasy of "mutedom." Verbal communication would definitely require more effort. I mean it's much easier to say something than write it down. I wondered how it would affect my need to control Terry. My guess is that it probably wouldn't take long to realize just how much I try to rearrange his thinking, manage his responses to suit me, or tell him how to do something.

When Terry finally moved the gearshift into third, I shot him the high sign with my right thumb. We were picking up speed now and, as sometimes happens in the fickle world of traffic, there appeared to be no apparent reason for the delay.

At 3:27 p.m., we drove through the E-Z pass tollbooth at the end of the turnpike. I hooked my hubby around the neck with the inside of my elbow and pulled him toward me. Then I kissed him on the cheek and went back to contemplating.

As an introvert, being a mute would be easy, *with conditions*. But to go out into the world, not care what other people think, and feel okay about it? That was the hurdle.

We hit a little traffic at the Delaware Memorial Bridge before we crossed the line into my home state of Maryland. It always feels good to be back, like wrapping a warm towel around my body when it's covered with goose bumps. Maryland, with the ocean and mountains and gentle hills and flat farmland, is known as "America in Miniature." When we passed over the rolling waters of the Susquehanna River, I thought about what we would find at the bottom of our oceans and rivers and lakes if they were drained.

I picked up the pad of paper again, which was now lying on the car floor at my feet.

I scribbled: *Are we in a hurry?*

Terry was driving 80 miles an hour but, then, so was everyone else. Some were even passing us. Controlling Terry is okay, I reasoned, when my personal safety was at risk.

The drive through the manicured, rolling farmland of northern Maryland is a welcomed stretch on 1-95. Only too soon, however, the box stores, housing developments, and business parks begin to appear as we get closer to Baltimore.

An older model black BMW moved into the lane in front of us with a Grateful Dead dancing bear sticker on the bumper. Jerry Garcia drove a black BMW around Marin County, California where he lived. I smiled. I could show up at a Dead concert with a little chalkboard strung around my neck and scribble away. There, I would fit in because no one would care, much less notice.

"So, why do you want to become a voluntary mute?" Terry finally asked.

He forgot that I don't like "why" questions. While most people don't seem to have any problem with them, they usually leave me feeling backed into a corner.

So, I wrote: *Say it differently.*

He thought for a moment. "Okay, so what makes you want to become a voluntary mute?"

I picked up my pen to answer his question and then put it down. It was too much to write. Later, after we got unpacked and settled in at home, I would tell him.

We were on Route 100, the last leg of our trip. It was 5:10 p.m. Eventually Route 100, a four lane divided highway, narrows down to two lanes and ends at the gatehouse where we live.

Some people believe that silence is the only true religion. Maybe I could start by not talking for one day. I could pick a day when I didn't teach yoga or have to go to the grocery store. Terry could take the dogs with him to work. But then, what's the point? In order to venture out of my comfort zone, I would have to pick a busy day and then just go for it.

At 5:35 p.m., we crossed the causeway to our little 1,000 acre island with its harbor on the right and the Chesapeake Bay on the left. Two miles from the gatehouse, as we drove down the driveway, I uttered my first words since we were on The Garden State Parkway over five hours ago.

"Ahhh. . .we're home."

Well behaved women rarely make history.
— Laurel Thatcher Ulrich

One world, one people, two sexes both equal,
twelve billion eyes, six billion souls see through them,
but just one race and that is human.

– Mr. Prophet

ONE

We are all one.

I t is with great curiosity that I find the "Blue Marble" photograph - the one of our planet suspended in outer *s p a c e* - the most requested picture of all time. Taken during the last mission of the Apollo flight program in December of 1972, the sun was behind the Apollo 17 spacecraft while it was traveling between the Earth heading towards the Moon. For personal reasons, this image of our planet effectively supports the concept that we are all one.

Even though we are born of the spiritual principle that we are all one, the challenge remains universal - we come armed with an ego that tries to seduce us from this truth. For example, I know that when I am judging others, I am also judging myself. What I believe, think, say, do, and feel is reflected back to me. Every relationship that I have mirrors some part of myself. All of this I get, yet I still see separateness.

Often, I ask myself what I have in common with suicide bombers, terrorist attackers, and murderers? I can't relate to people who kill for sport, drink urine, and get off on watching dog fights. As a woman, I don't understand the Islamic dress code, condoning bigamy, and those who stretch their neck with brass rings.

Yet, when I look at the now infamous photograph of Earth - or as Edgar Mitchell calls it "a glimpse of divinity" - I see no walls or war or white supremacy, just a big marble ball of Oneness. I see it, but in order to remember it, I sometimes have to go to that quiet place within. Like the astronauts' journey to outer *s p a c e*, getting there can take time especially if I am weighted down by the ego. But, when the gap between the thoughts finally widens and everything goes still inside, that's when I most feel the Oneness with all things.

This image of our planet also supports me when I need to put my life into perspective. With closed eyes, I imagine myself floating in outer *s p a c e,* interfacing with that beautifully illuminated silver dollar that we call Earth. There, I float in the reality that even with its challenges, sorrow, and pain, my life is truly blessed. I remember, with humility, that nothing seems as important as I thought it was and that I am merely a grain of sand among the many other trillion grains of sand.

Everyone has a soul purpose, we all speak the universal language of love, and all of us are connected to the same Source.

Yes, we are all one.

*Through compassion, you will find that all
human beings are just like you.*

– The Dalai Lama

My heart starts beating so fast...
it feels like it's going to explode.
My throat closes and I can't breathe.
I start to choke. My hands start sweating.
I get so dizzy I have to hold onto the furniture
or the wall to keep from falling or fainting.
I know I'm going to die.
I want to run, but I don't know where.

– anonymous

PHOBIAS

There's no other way to say it. I had a urinal phobia.

P hobias are defined as an intense fear of something that seemingly poses no threat or harm. The list is exhaustive, from ablutophobia (fear of washing or bathing) to zoophobia (fear of animals). The most common is social phobia, the fear of being evaluated negatively in social situations.

I know well the trauma that comes with phobias, having witnessed the devastating effect that a garden hose had on my friend, Lilly. Lilly was terrified of snakes, and seeing a black hose coiled up near my back door was enough to send her fleeing into my house. While her husband locked her in his arms, she heaved sobs of tears into his chest, her body shaking uncontrollably.

That day, Lilly decided to face her fear of snakes.

There are a number of ways to treat phobias. The most common is systematic desensitization, or exposure therapy, where the patient is exposed to the phobic stimulus. In some cases, results can be achieved in a single therapeutic session. Exposure therapy can be paired with the strengths of talk therapy and relaxation exercises to help patients become more aware of their feelings and behavior.

In Lilly's initial therapy session, she talked at great length about her fear of snakes before leaving with a homework assignment to visit the library and take out a book on them.

"It took me three days before I could even open it," Lilly told me over the phone.

At the next session, the therapist encouraged her to dine with her family at The Rattlesnake Grille, a local restaurant where she lived in Darien, Connecticut. Just pulling into the parking lot was going to be a challenge, but she did it. The following week, she rented a video about snakes. Every week, in addition to meeting with her therapist, her phobia became a little bit easier to tolerate until she was finally able to visit the reptile house at the zoo.

Lilly and I stayed in close touch during her very brave process. She has no memory of having been frightened by a snake, but she is an accomplished equestrian. I reminded her that a horse's worst fear is snakes.

"Maybe your horse was spooked by one while you were riding him," I suggested.

Like Lilly, I wasn't sure where the origin of my urinal phobia came from. As a woman, the chances of coming face to face with one is pretty remote. But, when I am caught off guard and stumble into a unisex bathroom that has a urinal, it feels like someone knocked the air out of my chest, causing me to flee like a refugee.

In addition to unisex bathrooms, there are some conferences where the facility has to open the men's room to accommodate the throngs of women. Or, the times when the ladies room is closed for repairs or cleaning and I have no choice but to use the men's bathroom.

Over the years, my reaction to the sight of a urinal was growing steadily worse. Finally, after encountering three urinals on three separate occasions in one week, I decided it was time to do something about it. So, through a referral, I found a therapist whose specialty was in treating phobias.

Sarah and I agreed to meet in her office the following Sunday, a day that would almost guarantee our being able to use the men's bathroom without being disturbed (or arrested). Initially, I talked about my phobia, sharing with her that I didn't have much to go on in terms of a connection to the source of my fear.

"I've even gone so far as to ask my friends - both male and female - if urinals frightened them."

Sarah said that we don't need to have a memory to treat a phobia, but sometimes it helps to know where it came from. She then explained her approach, what types of support were available, and ways to keep treating the phobia.

"Do you have any questions?"

I took a deep breath.

"Not at the moment."

She asked me to close my eyes before guiding me through a relaxation technique.

"This will help to ease your anxiety," she reassured me.

After a few minutes, she had me come out of the relaxation by opening my eyes. I felt calmer, although as we walked out of her office and down the long hall toward the men's bathroom, I felt a knot begin to tighten in my stomach again.

When we approached the bathroom door to the men's room, I asked her if she would go in first. I wanted to know how many urinals there were, where they were located, and whether they were floor or wall urinals. Floor urinals were scarier, a sign that the trauma probably happened when I was little and before mounted wall urinals were more common.

Sarah willingly agreed to go in before me. She looked around and, when she came back out, told me that there were two white wall units. They were behind a divider on the right side of the bathroom. On the left side were two sinks. On the other side of the sinks were two stalls.

"Okay," I told her, my body feeling rock hard. "I'm ready."

I latched onto her hand and, with closed eyes, took a conscious breath in and moved one foot forward. Then I took another breath and moved the other foot. I could already feel a deep sadness beginning to surface. After a few more steps, we made the u-turn around the divider to the right. My heart was pounding when we stopped. I opened my eyes and there they were, a pair of motionless white objects staring at me.

Knowing that I was there to face my fear, I wasted no time releasing the emotions that had been stored in my body all those years. With my head buried in Sarah's shoulder, I sobbed while she patiently held the s p a c e for me to feel the pain.

When the tears went dry, I sensed her moving away. She pulled some toilet tissue off of its roll and placed it in my hand. I blew my nose. Then, we stood in silence for a while.

Breaking the quiet, she asked me if I would be willing to touch one of the urinals.

I hesitated.

"They're disgusting, but I'll do it."

I touched the one on the left, the one that didn't have the chewed piece of gum near the drain. I moved a little closer. There was the faint smell of stale urine. Then, I touched the one on the right.

No longer did these cold, scary looking objects have any power over me. I was actually in a men's bathroom among the urinals in a state of calm surrender. I felt empty, the way I always do when I release a chunk of clutter, emotional or otherwise, from my life.

Sarah and I walked back to her office to wrap up our session. She encouraged me to keep visiting the car wash that I frequented, the one that had the unisex bathroom with the urinal. Before leaving, I told her that I still wanted to face my fear in front of a floor urinal, that there was something more to release.

"I can just feel it," I said.

Over the next few months, whether my car was dirty or not, I returned to the car wash bathroom. Even though I didn't love doing it, at least I could walk in without gasping for air.

At the time, I was working with an energy healer and mentioned my urinal phobia to her.

"Hey, I work in a bar on weekends that has one of those old floor urinals," Meg told me, wearing a riot of bright colors from her waist down. She reminded me of an old hippy with multiple piercings in her ears, long thick brown hair that needed combing, and tights under her skirt.

I laughed out loud, saying, "The Universe really does provide."

She offered to take me there one morning before the restaurant opened for lunch. We met the following week and sat down at the bar to talk first. I told her that it was much more frightening to approach a urinal from the right than it was from the left.

"Now, that's interesting," she said, crossing her legs before taking a sip of Perrier through a thin, ruby red bar straw.

Like Sarah, I asked Meg to describe the bathroom first.

"Well, it's the size of a small closet - one sink, one toilet, one urinal - big enough for one person."

Then she got up off of the bar stool, walked over to the door, and opened it.

"Let me know when you are ready," she said, adding, "Take your time."

I nodded, got up off the bar stool, and walked toward the door and stood about three feet away. I could see the urinal. Unlike the one at the car wash, this one had character with its stained, cracked marble and muted brass hardware. It was also situated so that I could only approach it from the right, the scarier side. Once again, the Universe provided the perfect scenario.

"What's going on?" Meg asked, sensing a shift in my energy.

While I stood there looking at the urinal, an image of Penn Station flashed across my mind. Interestingly, I had been there a few weeks before to pick up my mother and her husband on their way back from Florida. Baltimore's Penn Station was designed by New York architect Kenneth M. Murchison in the Beaux-Arts style, constructed in 1911 for about $1,000,000, and later renovated in stages beginning in the 1970's.

Maybe it was this recent visit to Penn Station that spawned a "sense" memory.

"I am with my father," I hear myself say.

Meg jumped right in.

"How old are you?" she asks.

"Little - two, maybe three years old.

"Go on."

"I am in the men's room at the train station. The bathroom has high ceilings, dark wood doors with white marble everywhere. I feel overwhelmed. "

The images continue to come.

"My father is facing the wall at the urinal. I am standing behind him and off to the right."

I am aware of my body, tightening like a boat covered in shrink-wrap. To keep the images alive, I close my eyes. I tell Meg that being a curious two year old, I move toward my father to see what he is doing. The next thing I know, there's a gigantic, hairy arm coming towards me.

"That must have been pretty scary," Meg says.

I told her that I became hysterical. Meg, her voice reduced to a whisper, gently reminded me that we are born with such delicate little nervous systems that it doesn't take much to traumatize us.

It was beginning to make sense - my father's arm was to protect me from seeing his penis. He didn't mean to scare me, but I was probably in the men's room because my mother wasn't with us. Still, there I was in the men's bathroom of the train station birthing a urinal phobia.

Phobias run in my family. When my mother was 10 years old, she watched a stray cat attack her mother, who was trying to shove some milk under a crawl *s p a c e* beneath their porch. Mother witnessed a sudden rush of gnashing teeth, wild eyes, and sharp claws, leaving my grandmother's face a bloody mess. As a result, Mother has suffered from a cat phobia ever since.

Avoiding her phobias didn't solve the problem. Wherever Mother went, there always seemed to be a cat at her feet. Once, she was conducting a board meeting for The March of Dimes in a private home where a cat was present. When Mother asked the hostess to remove it from the room, the woman never spoke to my mother again.

It didn't stop there. Years later, Mother was walking near her condo in Delaware when a cat jumped off of a wall and startled her. She reacted, fell, and broke her ankle.

"Once an alcoholic, always an alcoholic," Meg cautioned me that day. "You will probably never love being around urinals, but you have just minimized your fear of them immeasurably."

Like my mother's fear of cats, Lilly's fear of snakes, and mine to urinals, The Universe will keep putting the very thing that we are afraid of in front of us until we decide to deal with it.

The general public has always been skeptical regarding mental healing because it has never taken the pains to study the science which is its foundation. They believe it is easier to use medicine or surgery than to change basic subconscious patterns of belief and, for them, this is true.

— Raymond Charles Barker

People rarely disclose their character so
clearly as when they describe someone else's.

– unknown

RELATIONSHIPS

(Indented paragraphs in *italics* are from a talk given by Pastor Sam.)

Relationships are the most needful and most troubling things in our lives. We have an incredible need for relationships and nothing in our lives creates the source of complexity that they do.

These were the first words uttered from Pastor Sam Williams' mouth on the subject of voluntary simplicity at his church in Marin County, California. It was January 18, 1998, and I had the good fortune of visiting my sister the week of his talk titled, "Simplifying My Relationships: Enjoying the People I Love."

That Sunday, the simplicity disciple in me was hungry for any information that I could get my hands on, especially when it came to creating more satisfaction in the most challenging area of my life - relationships.

Pastor Sam drew me in immediately. He reminded me of Gerald Ford - distinguished and tall with sandy hair and looking fit in dark linen pants. What he possessed was born to him - charm, a mature heart and solid, good looks. His speaking skills were honed to perfection, making him easy to listen to.

Most of us have jobs, we live with people, and we can't get away from them. I love everything about my job, except for the people, and that's you.

Pastor Sam laughed, generating a few half-hearted chuckles from the audience, including me. As an introvert, I could relate to this. Some people I can live without, too.

*Simplicity is not about creating a whole other set
of rules and regulations about what the simple life is.
I suspect that will differ for everyone. What this is
about is an inward reality that results in an outward
lifestyle. How can I simplify what's <u>inside</u> my life.
How can I simplify my heart and my desires, for if I
can do that, then it is going to result in a lifestyle that
is more manageable and less complex. The outward
lifestyle is to love others as you love yourself, but it
begins with an inward reality.*

I used to think that simplifying my relationships meant
avoiding conflict, turning the other cheek to unacceptable
behavior, or choosing to abandon people altogether. I looked
over at my oldest younger sister, remembering the day a few
years back when she cried her way through the better part of an
afternoon reminding me of all the awful things that I had done
to her when we were growing up. She did it to heal herself, but
she also cared enough about me to want to repair our deeply
wounded relationship.

What my sister said was extremely painful to hear, but I was
able to give her the *s p a c e* to release her emotions until her last
tear was shed and, when it was over, the long process of healing for
us began. The rewards have been sweet. Today, she is one of my
best friends and, through her ability to forgive me, I am one of hers.

*We are the ones who have complicated our lives.
I suspect that the average person today sees more
people in a week than our great grandparents saw
in a year. I have a grandmother who never ventured
out of an eight block radius of her home. There are
some of us who live bi-coastal lives. Does that make
relationships complicated? I think so.*

Bi-coastal living would have been inconceivable to my grandparents, maybe even my parents. And, the mail? Today, we get more in one day than our great grandparents probably saw in a month.

I have come up with five categories of people. The first, I call the VRPs - the very resourceful people. These are the people who renew or ignite our passion, who draw out the best in us. For some of us, it was our parents. For others, it wasn't. It might be a close friend or a mentor, but it is somebody that when you are in their presence, it feels like a renewing experience because their life is so rich and their concern is so deep for you that it makes you want to be more than you are and draws out the very best in you. Now, if you have one person like that, hang on. It's not realistic to think that you would have a dozen people like this - one or two or three people in your life will generally suffice in this area, but it is important that you have one.

My VRP growing up was Marnie, my grandmother who loved me unconditionally. She was so spiritually connected and bursting with love for me that it would be hard to find anyone to fill her shoes. But she is gone now, so I decide its time to ask the Universe to help me attract another VRP into my life.

The second category of people I call VIPs - very important people. These are people who share my passion. They feel the way that I feel, they like what I like, they desire what I desire. These are the comrades, the people that I link arms with and work together with, and I would not be able to get done what I get done without these people. These are very important people.

I fare better in this category, having at least three or four people. However, if I could improve on one thing with my VIPs, it would be to spend more time with them.

The third category of people are the VTPs - very trainable people. Trainable people catch my passion. These are the people that want to learn from me. See, this is the reverse of the first relationship. In the first relationship, the very resourceful people, I am the trainable person. I am the sponge that's absorbing everything. The very trainable people want to learn from me. They are encouraged by my presence, and I am able to call out the best in them. It's important to have these relationships. In fact, these people help because these are the people that, if I do a good job with them, are going to be able to do what I am doing.

This was a challenge for me, mostly out of my need to control. In the ten years that I had my catering business, I was the owner, sales person, planner, bookkeeper, and chef. At parties, I didn't really want to relinquish any responsibility over to my crew because no one would be able to decorate the trays, pipe the filling for the deviled eggs, or arrange the flowers better than I could.

Now, it's at this point that I draw a dotted line, not a solid line because the purpose is to not live above the line. The dotted line is to make a distinction because these three categories above the dotted line are people that in one way or another simplify my life. The people below the line don't. This doesn't mean

*that they are bad people. Please understand that. It
means that I have a responsibility for maintaining
balance in my life between the people above the line
and the people below the line.*

I pulled some cinnamon gum from my satchel. It was my
favorite brand, Peelu. Even though it came in a little clear plastic box,
it didn't make up for the gum of my youth - Teaberry, Clove, and Black
Jack which my father used to chew for the sole purpose of flattening
it across his two front teeth to make it look like they were missing.

*The fourth category of people are VNPs - very
nice people. They enjoy my passion, they laugh at
my jokes, they applaud my efforts, they tell me what a
wonderful person I am, but they don't add anything to
my life. The drain here is almost all out. The danger
here is that you and I surround ourselves with very
nice people. These are the people who call and say,
"Can we get together for a little while," and you look
at your schedule and you say I don't want to do this
and then you remember how great they always say
you are. It's nice to have them around, but most of
us have too many of them in our lives.*

I'm sure that I maintain relationships with the very nice
people in my life because, as Pastor Sam said, they remember
my birthday, want to spend time with me, and usually take the
initiative to call. But, these relationships are also rooted in
obligation and, therefore, will rarely feel like an even exchange of
energy. Now that I understand why my relationships with VNP's
are unsatisfying, I can release some of them from my life. Of
course, I must also humble myself by saying that I am a very nice
person on someone else's list.

The last category are the VDPs - the very draining people. These are the people who sap my passion. I tell you, I think it works the same on both ends of the scale. If there are only one or two people that you and I are likely to have for very resourceful people, then I don't think many of us can manage more than one or two VDPs in our lives. I think you will discover that if you are tired, really, really tired, and you have lost your passion for your job, for your family, for your friends, I think if you will analyze your schedule and look at the people you spend time with, you'll find that it is weighed down with the very nice people and the very draining people, and they have crowded out the very resourceful people in your life and almost excluded the very trainable people because that always boils down to 'I can always get around to them.'

It's inevitable that we are going to have draining situations and people in our lives. I have had my share, some of whom I won't abandon - a friend who is going through a crisis, a sick family member, or someone who needs my time. However, all is not lost in this category. As Carl Jung says, "Everything that irritates us about others can lead us to an understanding of ourselves."

So how do these people affect this issue of simplicity? The very resourceful people simplify my life because they renew me, they give me the energy to get back at it. They give me the insight I need to do what I'm doing and, without these people, our lives will become complicated because I'm not getting the resources I need to do the things I need to do.

*The very important people simplify my life
because they encourage me in what I am doing. I'm
not doing it by myself. I don't feel alone. And I don't
overwork because I've got people who are important
in my life that share the work load with me.*

*The very trainable people simplify my life
because, if I am investing my life in them, then they
are going to be able to do what I am doing and they
are going to be able to carry on what I am doing.*

*The very nice people complicate my life because
they take my time and energy, but they don't return
anything. They aren't trying to wear us out. They just
like being around us. Again, the only problem is that
there are too many of them.*

*And the very draining people? It's obvious, I
guess, how they complicate our lives because their
lives are so complicated. If you found out that you
only had three hours to live, these are the people you
would want to be with because three hours with them
seems like a lifetime.*

Pastor Sam laughed, a hint of compassion in his voice.

*These are people who need friends, and they
need help, and their lives are very, very complicated.
But you and I can only manage one or two of them,
and the inability to say "no," the inability to be
discerning , and the inability to be wise complicates
life and wears us out.*

*Simplicity. I simplify my life by understanding
the roles that people have that are part of my life.
How I relate to them and how they relate to me. And*

maintaining a balance in my relationships so that, yes, I'm not an unconcerned, uncaring person who is unwilling to be involved in other people's lives. There are some very draining people in my life. They are ministries, and that's okay and I am called to that. In fact, we are called to give ourselves to some people without expectation of anything in return, but if that defines my life, then my life is going to be unbelievably complicated. My life cannot be defined by one kind of person. It's got to have balance to it.

The more you go towards the top of the category list, the more intentional you have to be, the more you have to seek out and nurture those relationships. The nice people and the draining people will seek you out. You will need to seek out the trainable people, the important people, and the resourceful people. It's an initiative that you need to make in order to maintain the balance. In my mind, the balance is above and below the dotted line and you and I have got to intentionally create the balance because the nice and draining people are going to be there anyway.

Now, the same person can move from one category to another. You see, your children can be very important people or very trainable people until they become teenagers and then they can become very draining people. They take everything out of you and put nothing back and then, because somebody has moved categories, somebody else has got to be brought into your life to create the balance.

I realized the "one in, one out" guideline isn't just for possessions, but can be used in all areas of our lives.

*Second suggestion for you this morning.
Simplify your relationships by simplifying your
speech. And, this may be the sneaker; this may be
the one that seems too simple, but it might have the
greatest impact. Simply let your "yes" be "yes" and
your "no" be "no." Say what you mean, mean what
you say. Tell the truth. Don't create fancy language
to make it appear that you're saying one thing when
you mean something else. The complexity and the
confusion in our relationships is due in large part to
the fact that we don't speak plainly. I didn't say ugly.
It is possible to speak plainly and speak with great
compassion and concern.*

Pastor Sam really nailed it. This is about much more
than not just telling a lie. For many of us, it's uncomfortable to be
open and transparent in our relationships. We don't share what
we really feel and the consequences of those decisions complicate
our lives. People with integrity know this and aren't afraid to cut
through all of the verbal clutter.

*Our lives and our relationships would be so much
simpler if we just shared with each other what we feel
and think, what we need and desire.*

He looked at the clock on the wall. I noticed that the talk
was going over the allotted time, but I didn't care. I could have
listened to him all day.

Then, he closed with the following story:

*When my children were very young preschoolers,
I started a new job, and it was a very challenging job,*

and I was so excited about it that I was giving myself completely to it and not spending any time with my family. The time that they got, I was very drained. I was always making promises about when I would be home and what I would do with them and I was regularly missing those expectations. One night, I was going to meet Nancy and the kids at a pizza place for dinner. Well, some very nice person needed to see me and I couldn't say "no" to nice people because they were telling me what a wonderful pastor I was. "We've never had a pastor like you, Pastor Sam." And how do you say "no" to people like that? So, I got to the pizza place about an hour and a half late. When they weren't there, I asked the kid who was working if there was a woman, a nice looking woman, with two little kids.

"Yeah," the kid said, "they already had their pizza and left."

Well, I got home and said to Nancy, "Why did you leave the pizza parlor. I told you I was coming," and so on and so forth.

So, we began a serious conversation. And it ended something like this. Nancy said to me, "I'm not going to tell you what to do. All I hope is that twenty years from now your children will love you as much as your church does. And I'm not sure that they will if they don't see any more of you."

And then she just left it. She didn't tell me what to do. It's hard to fight with somebody who doesn't tell you what to do. And I was forced to face the truth about myself.

Nancy told me that everything has been said, that we're not going to talk about it anymore. She

*reminded me that it was my decision. That was twenty
years ago and I don't know how much you like me, but
my kids love me.*

*So, how do you get that kind of relationship?
You don't get it in a day. It comes over time, from
prioritizing. It comes by maintaining a balance in
your life so that the people who are important know
that they are important, and you choose to make
room and time for them.*

On the flight home from California, I took an inventory
of my relationships. It was evident that there were too many
people below the line and not enough above it. Over the next few
months, I found the hardest group of people to let go of were
the very nice people. When I would no longer engage the very
draining people, they eventually slid into obscurity and found
someone else who would listen to their problems.

Just as Pastor Sam promised, the most challenging
relationships to cultivate and maintain are with those people above
the line. These are the ones who draw me out of my comfort
zone and force me to show up in life. These are the relationships
that afford me the opportunity to make deeper, more meaningful
connections, not only with others, but with myself.

**Let me remember that each life must follow its own course,
and that what happens to other people has absolutely nothing
to do with what happens to me.**

— Marjorie Holmes

Our thoughts become our prayers;
to worry is to pray for what you don't want.

– Reverend Amalie

REVEREND AMALIE

Off and on for over four decades, I wrestled with a lot of things, but not like I did when it came to understanding God. As a child, while my parents paid penance for their sins, I was belting out "Jesus Loves Me" in the basement of our local Presbyterian church. It was a futile attempt because, even when I sang loud, I never felt His love.

Worse, God looked like a Diane Arbus version of Father Time who hovered from above and never slept. Most days, I would wake up and wonder how I was going to get through the day without committing a sin. It was all so confusing and full of conflict that when I left home for college, I was happy to give up the struggle to figure it out.

Then, in the summer of 1972, while Olga Korbut strutted her stuff across the balance beam in Munich, I smoked marijuana for the first time in a pup tent on the sand dunes of Nantucket Island. From the moment I took a hit off of that joint, all doubt was erased. My mind settled, my body felt electrified. I was outgoing and funny. People liked me, listened to my brilliant ideas, even applauded my polished opinions.

But the high would never last long enough for me, nor could I hold onto it. Instead, I was left feeling tired, lonely, disappointed and, worse, wanting to feel good again. So began a long, tempestuous relationship with pot and alcohol in order to re-create that experience on Nantucket.

Fifteen long years later, I finally surrendered my tattered soul to Alcoholics Anonymous and, with it, the sleepwalking phase of my life ended. Since the foundation of A.A. is a spiritual one, I began to re-evalute my religious concepts, beliefs, and ideas. In order to make that happen, I had to dismantle them in order to open up the *s p a c e* to find my Truth.

It was in A.A. that I first heard about the concept of a higher power. For these folks in recovery, it was about the God of each person's understanding. No one cared what your label of choice was, and the black sheep in me liked that.

"I see Spirit in my cat," one woman confessed, knitting methodically through a web of yellow yarn.

Standing in the back of the crowded room, a seasoned veteran shared that the God of his understanding was in the messages that he heard in the rooms. "In the rooms" is A.A. lingo; whatever is said in the rooms stays in the rooms.

Eventually, I chose a name for the God of my understanding - "H.P.", short for higher power. It sounded hip, not religious, so as not to scare anyone off outside of the rooms. Still, the little kid in me couldn't abandon the "bearded man in the sky" until I had something to replace Him with.

So, I sat in the park and stared at the trees, looking for my "H.P." like a long lost pal. Often, I would fantasize about seeing a vision of white light standing at the foot of my bed at night. In the rooms of A.A., I continued to gather ideas, one meeting at a time, while waiting for my very own spiritual awakening.

I also tried numerous non-denominational churches, rebirthed under water, and listened to spiritual tapes in the car. I attended new age healing seminars, meditation groups, even walked grass labyrinths in the front yards of private homes. I talked to my therapist about God and kept on searching.

It was during this time that the Church of Religious Science found me, a new thought religion that teaches, among other things, that our thinking creates our reality, that Jesus is the example - not the exception - and that we are one with God.

A few weeks later, on April 2, 2000, Reverend Amalie Frank was invited to be the guest speaker at this church. Arriving with her young boy driver who, I might add, was very cute, she stepped out of a black Town Car clutching a copy of her book *Reverend Amelia's Good Words - Signposts for the Journey.*

Born in 1910, Amelia H. Frank was schooled at Peabody Conservatory of Music, Johns Hopkins University, and the University of Maryland before teaching Music and English in the Baltimore City school system. After retiring, she became an ordained Unity minister in October 1976. In her second career, she would grow numerous fledgling churches before retiring at the age of 87.

Even at five feet tall, Reverend Amalie had presence, like a bonsai tree in a cathedral. Her eyes were patient; the lines on her face a canvas of kindness. She looked like someone who smiled in her sleep.

Through an informal introduction that Sunday morning, we learned that Reverend Amalie's personal life, like her academic and teaching career, was a palate of varied interests. She had four children, nine grandchildren, and sixteen great grandchildren. In her spare time, what little of it there was, she read racy, romantic novels. At the age of 67, she flew a Cessna 150 solo. One story goes that when a traffic court judge gave her a warning instead of a fine, he cautioned Amalie to "stop driving her age."

Now, instead of standing behind the lectern to speak, she marched right out into the audience - all eighty pounds of her. I remember that her message was crisp, animated, and very funny.

"God is in this floor," she said, pointing to the floor. "God is in the ceiling. God is in those plants. God is in the program that you are holding."

Now, in the back of my mind, I couldn't quite get my arms around God being in the linoleum floor beneath me. But when I thought about it later, it made sense that if the raw materials came from God, and God is in man, and man laid the floor, then God could be in the floor.

After running her tongue across the front of her teeth, she went on.

"God is in the person sitting next to you."

I looked over at my husband Terry who was picking the wart on the top of his right hand. Some days, I had to work real hard to see God in him.

Amalie paused to look around the room.

"Picture an ocean. Is there any place in the ocean where there is no water?"

I looked around the room, where a crowd of 100 were sitting neatly in rows of 10.

"It's the same with God. There is no place in the Universe where God isn't. God is everywhere. God is in the breath that breathes you. God is in you."

That's when the flash-bulb went off and, with it, forty-seven years of searching was distilled into one beautiful moment of Truth. I have always been a part of the whole.

"You are God's creation, an expression of Divinity in human form," she said. "You are a chip off the old block."

After the service was over, I bought a copy of Amalie's book, sharing with her the impact of her message. I thanked her for reminding me that everything we need is within. I wanted to stay longer and hold her vein-splattered hand, but there was a line of people behind me waiting to have their books signed, too.

After turning to leave the room, I stepped through the church door and opened the book. On the inside cover, she had written: "To Kater, with love and thanks. Amalie."

Three years later, on New Year's Eve, Reverend Amalie died at the age of 93.

The difference between great people and everyone else
is that great people create their lives actively,
while everyone else is created by their lives,
passively waiting to see where life takes them next.
The difference between the two is the difference between
living fully and just existing.

— Michael Gerber

If there is something that you desire and it is not coming to you, it always means the same thing. You are not a vibrational match to your own desire.

– Abraham-Hicks

SIGNS

It was the swing under the tulip magnolia in the front yard that was my sign. Immediately, I stopped my car to take a closer look. It was a turquoise plastic swing, the bucket type large enough to hold a toddler. To the left of the swing, and down a gradual slope about fifty yards away, stood the playhouse.

I shifted my focus back to the child's swing. Behind it was the main house, a traditional home built in the late forties. The exterior was made of stone and wood with black shutters and a slate roof. I noticed a green Honda sedan parked at the top of the driveway.

I turned the ignition off and opened the passenger window. This was the house where I had grown up and, in the eighteen years since my parents sold it, the property had changed hands twice.

I never met the owners who bought the house from my parents, but Mother told me that my father bounced their baby on his knee for the entire three hour settlement. The former owners, whom I will name Mr. and Mrs. Sink - an acronym for single income no kids - were an older couple, he about twenty years her senior.

I got the Sinks' telephone number from a former neighbor. After calling to introduce myself, I asked her if she would take me through the house where my family had lived for over three decades. The call was brief, I recall, with just enough time to arrange a date and time.

The following week, I was standing at her front door. When she opened it, I immediately felt uneasy. A heavyset woman with a slight limp and black, unruly hair, she wasted no time once I stepped into the foyer and took my coat off. Moving from room to room, she made no mention of the exquisite woodwork that my father built (some of which came from the mansion of the famous architect, Stanford White, after it was torn down in Baltimore), the clever way that he created storage *s p a c e*, or all the stone masonry that he laid in the backyard. But, in all fairness to her, she didn't have the same emotional attachment that I did either.

I noticed there were things that had been ripped out, like the outdoor kitchen that Dad built and the small corner bookshelves on the landing at the top of the stairs. A beautiful old dutch door had been removed in the upstairs sewing room, as well as a wooden door in the downstairs family room. That door was replaced with an ugly, off-white shear curtain.

As we wandered into my childhood bedroom, Mrs. Sink mentioned that they also owned a working horse farm north of Baltimore, as well as a summer place located in tony Edgartown on Martha's Vineyard. Now, the house where my family of seven lived on with an acre of land, a stream, woods, and a swimming pool was a mere pied a' terre for them.

And then, of course, there was the playhouse. Built by my father in 1975, it drew even more attention than the original one (see the picture on p. 143). Through the years, numerous stories had been written about it in the local, as well as national, newspapers.

"Mr. Leatherman," one article wrote, "took a stick to draw the line in the dirt for the foundation and put up the first two-by-four for the right hand corner. Working with no more plans than he could carry in his head, stepping back now and then to get a good view of the main house, he created this miniature version of the outside of his own home at one-quarter scale; it is 27 feet long, 6 feet deep and 7-1/2 feet high. The playhouse is an exact replica of the main house. Exact to the extent of duplicate burglar alarms, landscaping, paint jobs and lamps. The likeness is startling in the painstaking attention paid to the slightest detail."

After Mrs. Sink and I walked down the stairs and out the breakfast room door, we headed down the hill along the edge of the asphalt driveway to the miniature house.

I told her that my father used no architectural plans to build it.

"Oh? "

"One local architect took photographs of it and made slides to teach his students the concept of scale. He joked that Dad was going to put architects out of business."

She seemed unaffected.

Now, the shutters on the playhouse were falling off and the garage window had been knocked out. The fake stone facade and wood siding were deteriorating.

"You know," I said to her, holding back the tears, "How would you feel if I raised the money to have it restored?"

. . . .

A few weeks later, I dropped off an old collage of black and white photographs taken when the backyard swimming pool was built in the spring of 1968. I also included a framed timeline of the pool project, handwritten in calligraphy, that included the assassination of Martin Luther King on April 4. The pictures and timeline really belonged in the bathhouse that my father and grandfather built. That day, the Sinks weren't home, so I put everything by the front door and left, never to hear from them again.

Three years later, when I drove past the house and saw the turquoise swing under the tulip magnolia, it was obvious that something had changed. The yard looked well tended, not bordering on neglect like before. Even though the playhouse was in the same condition, there was a little wreath on the front door.

The Ruxton playhouse with the main house behind it.

I put the passenger window up and pulled into the driveway and parked behind the green Honda sedan. Instead of knocking on the front door, I went to the breakfast room door, just like I did growing up.

My heart was pounding when I tapped on it lightly. Inside, I could hear the sound of a children's television show. After a few seconds lapsed, the door opened. There she stood, a vision of blonde freshness, probably in her late thirties, standing slender at 5'7" tall with her hair pulled back in a ponytail. She was also talking on the phone.

She gently placed her hands over the mouthpiece.

"May I help you?"

I very quickly told her who I was and that I had grown up in the house. She flashed a warm smile, let me in immediately, and told whoever was on the phone that she would call them back later.

"Hi, I'm Diana DeVeas."

. . . .

Two weeks later, I returned with my younger brother and sister to see Diana and meet her husband, Willie. They met in dental school, where the pair worked on the same cadaver. Willie, an affable guy with a smile only a dentist could have, filled the foyer with his frenetic energy. He, like Diana, was generous in welcoming the three of us back to our childhood home.

"We absolutely love this place," Willie told us as we moved toward the dining room. "When we first looked at the house, I knew it was the one. Then we walked into the living room and saw the swimming pool through the picture window. That's when I turned to the realtor and told him to make it happen."

On September 11, 2000, this family with two young children, moved in. After living there for a few months, Willie told us that he discovered the dumbwaiter that my father had built, along with a pocket door in the master bedroom that had been painted shut. Diana unearthed a walkway along the side of the house that was overgrown with weeds. In the bathhouse loft, they found a very dusty black and white picture collage and pool timeline that I had dropped off to Mrs. Sink three years earlier.

"This place has been like an archeological dig," Diana told us.

As we ventured out into the backyard, I showed them some photographs of the outdoor kitchen before it had been demolished. The pool looked the same except that the diving board was gone. So was the treehouse that my father built for my younger brother.

From there, we went back inside and filed down the stairs into the family room where my parents had transformed a 50's club basement with knotty pine walls and vinyl floors into a cozy, comfortable place to relax, cook, entertain, and eat. The rustic style kitchen had also been featured in a Baltimore Sun article titled, "The House with Three Kitchens." In the family room, almost everything was the way that I remembered it, except for extensive water damage to the wood floor near the fireplace.

Midway through our visit, we moved up to the first floor again where Diana had set out a colorful spread with finger sandwiches, bow pasta salad, and assorted cookies. We barely made a dent, especially since it was enough for twenty-five

The back of the playhouse. So as not to make it overly cute, my father decided not to install a miniature swimming pool.

people. I also remember how strange it felt to ask her if I could use the bathroom.

After lunch, we went to the second floor where Diana, like my mother, kept a flower arrangement in the niche near the stairs. Mittens, hats, and scarves were stored in the same cubby. They even kept their luggage in the identical storage closet that was right next to my brother's bedroom.

Diana and Willie so loved and appreciated my father's craftsmanship that I felt like my childhood home had come full circle. The DeVeas were even the same age as my parents when they purchased the house in 1957.

Finally, I said to Diana and Willie, "Let's go down and see the playhouse."

Three months later, the SAVE THE PLAYHOUSE campaign was launched. I mailed over 125 letters to Dad's family and business acquaintances, my parents' friends, and long time residents of the community.

In the letter, I wrote that the contractor would have to painstakingly dismantle the exterior before replacing the windows, molding, stonework, shutters, and roof. The work would take approximately three months and cost $10,000 (it took much longer and cost twice as much). All contributors would have their name printed on a plaque to be placed on the property. They would also be invited to a celebration party upon its completion.

Within days, donations started pouring in. The former Mayor of Baltimore, an advocate for preservation and a friend of my father's, made two separate contributions. Some gave on the spot when I told them about the project. One local landscaping company offered to mulch, plant shrubs, and reseed the area in front of the playhouse.

The list goes on.

In hindsight, Mrs. Sink's attitude and lack of interest in the restoration was a red flag. To work on this project with them probably wouldn't have been easy or fun. On the other hand, I was getting all the signs that Diana and Willie would be there to support me, cooperate in any way possible, and show their appreciation. In both cases - with the Sinks and the DeVeas - there was a divine hand in the till.

Many of us grow up with the message that in order for something to have value, it has to be hard, that we must sweat, struggle, and sacrifice for it. Or, if something is easy, then somehow we don't deserve it. When things are meant to be, there is a sense of ease, of being in the flow, of feeling supported by a force much more powerful than we are.

My job in restoring the playhouse was to maintain faith, focus, and footwork. Naturally there were challenges, but ideas and solutions came easily, money showed up when I needed it, and people came to help at the perfect time.

Signs are all around us if we are paying attention. They come from people, song lyrics, our intuition, billboards, license plates, bumper stickers, being in nature, and more. Seeing one is God's gift to us. Taking action is the gift that we give to ourselves.

Anthony Robbins reminds us that, "In life, lots of people know what to do, but few people actually do what they know. Knowing is not enough. You must take action." The turquoise swing in the front yard was my sign that the house was occupied by a new owner. But I had to knock on the door to find out if there was any possibility of restoring the playhouse.

After Diana placed the cordless phone on the kitchen counter that first day and introduced herself, she looked at me and said, "Do you know how long I have been waiting for someone in your family to knock on our door?"

It was a sign that was definitely meant to be.

*I feel there are two people inside of me –
me and my intuition.
If I go against her, she'll screw me every time,
and if I follow her, we get along quite nicely.*

– Kim Basinger

It's a paradox:
Abundance comes from emptying ourselves
of not feeling, being, or having enough.

– the author

STAYING RID
OF MATERIAL CLUTTER

I n the decade leading up to the new millennium, simplicity finally went mainstream and clutter became the "it" word in households across America. The surge of information came quickly, I remember, and folks were buying books by the millions. There were workshops on clearing clutter with feng shui, magazine articles about creating more s p a c e, and talk shows on how to live simply.

So, with great enthusiasm, many of us forged ahead, either choosing to give away or toss out possessions before reorganizing what was left. We discovered that we felt lighter, more energized, and less stressed. Yes, for the most part, it felt good to purge.

And then clutter - or what I call the "sneak thief" of life - resurfaced, reminding us that staying on top of clutter requires maintenance. However, with a little practice, keeping it under control can become as automatic as brushing your teeth. Even if you haven't jumped on the bandwagon to conquer clutter, you can begin by setting your intention.

Remember, it takes 21 days to integrate a new habit into your life *if you do it every day.* Here are twelve ways to practice "discardia" and maintain a clutter-free life:

1. Empty trash daily as a reminder to stay rid of clutter. Handle the mail when it comes in and open it over the trash. Discard the junk and sort what's left into piles. Stage mail for family members in their office, cubbyhole, or bedroom. Put magazines, newspapers, and catalogs where you will read them. File bills in a folder.

2. Write things down. Having your "to do" list floating around in your head is a form of mental clutter that can hinder your ability to relax and enjoy life.

3. Strive to become a conscious consumer. Before you buy something, ask yourself: "Do I really need this? Want it? Love it? Is it going to complicate or simplify my life? Will it take up too much s p a c e, either physically, emotionally, or mentally?

4. Say yes to yourself by saying no to others if you don't want something, even if it belonged to a family member. Once you accept it, then you are stuck with the difficult task of getting rid of it.

5. Ask for gifts that won't clutter your home such as a certificate for a massage, coupon book for big screen movies, restaurant voucher, theater or museum pass, or concert ticket(s).

6. When practical, instead of buying, rent or borrow equipment, books, and movies.

7. When donating to charitable fundraisers, kindly pass on those incentive gifts if you don't want them.

8. Send a handwritten thank you note in lieu of a "hostess" gift to avoid cluttering up other peoples' homes.

9. Commit to going through your house at least once a year. Basements, lofts, attics, garages, desks, drawers, closets, and pocketbooks are all magnets for clutter. Make four piles - keep, sell, donate, and discard. Then sort, rearrange, clean, and put the rest away.

10. To maintain control, adopt the "one in, one out" guideline when adding things to your life. Put things back where they belong. Clear accumulated clutter from your house every time the seasons change. Examples would include getting rid of last month's magazine when the new one arrives or giving away one pair of unused shoes when you buy new ones.

*Habits...the only reason they persist is that
they are offering some satisfaction...
You allow them to persist by not seeking any other,
better form of satisfying the same needs.*

*Every habit, good or bad, is acquired and learned
in the same way - by finding that it is
a means of satisfaction."*

— Juliene Berk

Stress is nothing more than a
socially acceptable form of mental illness.

– Richard Carlson

STRESS

Today, I am on a voyage through the southern Caribbean via a large passenger ship. Here, on the Atlantic Ocean, my stress level is at the low end of the spectrum. While it is easy to stay balanced on this "home" away from home, I will inevitably wrestle with behaviors that cause me stress once the vacation is over.

Stress is the human body's natural instinct to defend itself. While it seems like circumstances outside of ourselves cause the most stress, most suffering comes from the s p a c e between our ears - our self-induced thoughts, attitudes, and perceptions. Any overload spreads to our body and manifests as physical illness.

Repressed emotions, such as anger and resentment, also cause stress. For some, stress comes with an element of excitement that can also feel energizing and addictive, a quality that may cause us to create more of it. Adding to the stack that takes its toll on our health and well-being are the mundane as well as exotic events in our day to day lives.

There are some not so obvious stressors, including the inability to take responsibility. If you live from a place of blessing instead of blame, you will clear s p a c e for change by stimulating new energy, personal power, and inner growth.

On the following page are twenty-six ways, one for each letter of the alphabet, to help you minimize the effects of stress in your daily life:

Avoid toxic thinking

Breathe deeply

Challenge your perceptions

Dwell in the solution

Exercise

Feel your feelings

Get support

Humor

Imagine, or "image-in" a different outcome

Just remember that not all will get done

Keep it simple

Listen to music that you love

Make peace with your shortcomings

No is saying yes to yourself

Opt to let go

Play

Question your motive(s)

Read something uplifting

See the innocence in others; most people are doing their best

Take responsibility for your actions

Unwind in the bathtub

Visualize the bigger picture

When in doubt, sleep on it

Xerox a copy of this and keep it visible

Yoga to release tightness and tension

Zone out for a 20 minute power nap

Reality is the leading cause of stress amongst those in touch with it.

– Jane Wagner

THE FIVE GIVENS OF LIFE:

1. *Everything changes and ends.*
2. *Things do not always go according to plan.*
3. *Life is not always fair.*
4. *Pain is part of life.*
5. *People are not loving and loyal all the time.*

– David Richo

STRIPPED

... at fifty-six.

Some believe that every seven years we experience a major change, a kind of metamorphosis or an awakening to another part of ourselves. My life, in this eighth cycle, was about love and loss and letting go. In 2008, I met a man who, in five brief months, impacted my life more than all the others combined.

I saw him first, on a mundane Monday morning, standing just inside the gym. He was distracted with his BlackBerry wearing black sweatpants, a baseball cap, and wire rim glasses. At 5'7" - a couple inches taller than me - he was stocky with olive skin, a belly full of fat, and looking very huggable. Those who knew me probably wouldn't pick him out as a match, but the chemistry was there.

When he finally looked up and flashed an infectious smile, our relationship officially took off. Clearly, in our initial conversation, he was drawn in by my commitment to live simply - eliminating tolerations, toxic people and finding ways to create more *s p a c e* in life. I loved his "Italian-ess," sense of humor, and impeccable integrity. He told me that he had a grown daughter, was a lawyer, ran the court system in a major East Coast city for six years, and loved to cook.

The two of us moved quickly into what we called our "besotted phase," a fusion of euphoria and intensity. He would tell me, and anyone who would listen, how beautiful and talented and amazingly wonderful I was. I, in turn, would tie the shoelaces on his Nubucks, cover his hands with adoring kisses, and sit by his feet - just like Katharine Hepburn did with Spencer Tracy.

Sometimes, we would stagger around the grocery store, holding each other up by our wits - our bodies lined up perfectly - with no shopping list or menu plan or clue as to what we needed to buy. Then, with the accelerating tension of sexual possibility pulsing through our veins, we went home to celebrate our love - urgent, insatiable - until finally everything went still inside, the dull and shallow world falling away around us.

When we weren't together, I slept next to my computer and he with his BlackBerry.

"R U Awake?" I would write at 3 a.m.

"Yes, thinking of you."

Four months after we met, he invited me to come and live with him.

"I can just see you here," he confessed, taking pictures of me one right after the other while I moved my besotted self in circles around his kitchen.

In an e-mail a couple of days later, he wrote: "What will it take?"

On June 7th, I moved in, just shy of five months after we met.

We gleefully "played house" for about three weeks until, all too painfully soon, it became evident that our shared s p a c e (including my two dogs) was too cramped for us. The fact that we both worked from home didn't help either. I was gaining weight - to the tune of 10 pounds in four months - consuming his delectable homemade pasta, bread, and pizza. He was also striving to adjust to the many changes, which included living with someone who was also set in her ways. But it was our difference in lifestyles that ultimately forced us to separate amicably after only nine weeks.

Other losses would follow. I gave up one of my dogs. Thirteen days later, my beloved uncle - a father figure and the funniest, most lovable man I've ever known - died. At his memorial service, my ex-husband showed up with my former sister-in-law, the woman he had fallen in love with while we were married. Then one of my oldest and closest girlfriends turned trans-male. By this time, in dire need of some nurturing, I called to get a haircut and discovered my hairdresser's number had been disconnected. After a 35 year relationship, now he too was gone, having mysteriously disappeared off the face of the earth.

But, the most painful loss was the unexpected separation from my lover of five months, even though we talked about dating after I moved out. The *s p a c e* that his absence left caused me to collapse into a state of grief so intense that it felt like Hannibal Lecter had descended over me. With the swish of a horse's tail, all of his affection, attention, appreciation, and acceptance was gone from my life.

I lost my appetite and shed the weight I had gained while we were together. Some days, in order to embrace the pain, I forced myself to sit on my hands to avoid distracting myself with food or television. Then, in the cruel dead of the night, I would wake up feeling nauseous before the inevitable tornado whirling around my head kicked in. I became sleep deprived.

I knew that 80% of my grief had to do with my past - the abandonment, the loss, and not feeling good enough as a kid. The other 20% had to do with the present situation. And there he was, holding up the mirror to shine the light on my old, still unresolved wounds. Over the years, I had done alot of work around these very same issues but, clearly, this was another layer, a much deeper layer.

This time during my life "in the well" moved very slowly, like watching a frozen steak thaw on the kitchen counter. Teaching yoga and writing sustained me, but in my deep longing to connect with him, I remembered how desperately lonely I felt as a kid. Then I cried for all the things that could have been, including my childhood and how it would have been different had my father not been an alcoholic and my mother so distant, narcissistic and controlling.

I returned to Al-Anon, where I heard the slogans that helped me treat my codependency over two decades before - let go and let God, changed attitudes can aid recovery, one day at a time, this too shall pass. I spent time with friends, prayed, and continued to process my wellspring of emotions.

One evening, I went through my books and pulled one from the shelf. It was Sara Davidson's book, *LEAP! What Will We Do with the Rest of Our Lives? Reflections From the Boomer Generation.*

In it, she talks about a woman, Marion Woodman, who had suffered from "a terrible anguish of the soul." After hearing a tape about her story, Davidson interviewed her over the telephone.

"Everything I'd known was being stripped from me," Woodman shared with her, "This can be a time of multiple blows. Your body is losing its beauty and strength, the kids are not turning out the way you had hoped, your partner is gone."

Davidson herself was going through the same thing, including a breakup with her lover, someone she "couldn't seem to untangle from her body and missed him so intensely that she wanted to call and tell him he could name his terms, just come back." In addition, her livelihood had stalled and her two grown children had moved out.

Woodman tells Davidson, in their phone interview, that these periods of loss can occur between the ages of fifty-five and sixty, but she's seen it happen at forty.

"When it does," Woodman says, "you have to ask yourself, why am I being stripped? You may think: I'm lost, I don't want to struggle on. I don't like what I see in the mirror. I'd rather die in full flight. Then a new energy comes and says: I am going to live."

The comfort I get from reading this causes me to weep. Stripping can happen to anyone and, while I have felt despair, there seems to be an indomitable thread of strength that will get me through this emotional tsunami.

What Davidson didn't prepare me for was the unforeseeable loss of my old self, as well as my old life before I met him. Nothing felt the same. Television shows that I used to watch no longer held the same appeal. Instead of flipping through magazines, I wanted to read books. Before I was rarely lonely; now I needed to get out and connect with people. I stopped the laborious task of dehydrating food and simplified my diet and, more surprisingly, discovered that I wasn't as controlling and meticulous as I used to be.

I continued to grieve, crying on the bathroom floor, my cheek pressed against the cold, tile floor. I wept in my walk-in closet with the lights off and the door shut while my dog, Sweet Potato, licked my tear-stained face. Sometimes, in the middle of the night - unable to sleep - I would walk to the community gym and peddle my tears out on the exercise bike.

I was being led to the truth through the breakdown of my illusions, of how I thought my life would turn out and what I believed love was. Already, I had suffered through two failed marriages and now, thinking I would spend the rest of my life with this man - "the third's the charm" - what was left for me if I couldn't make this work?

Eventually, I found the strength to journal my gains. Returning my dog, Kiwi, to my ex-husband was unbearable, but it helped heal our thirteen-year marriage and now Sweet Potato is much happier living alone with me. When my hairdresser disappeared, I found someone who cut my hair in a new, more stylish way. And, after my uncle died, a man whose religion was humor, I got a call to teach a laughter yoga class, something I had been certified to do six months before.

In addition, there was the nightmare of having to move twice in nine weeks, but my one bedroom apartment facing the woods is more calming to my soul than the two bedroom I had overlooking a busy marina. And, of course, there was the gift of having met him. Even with a broken heart, this beautiful man who I wouldn't have chosen in a lineup brought me out of my shell, unleashed my passion, and opened my heart in ways that I had never felt before.

Six months after we separated, I could feel myself coming out of what Carolyn Myss calls "the dark night of the soul." I had befriended pain and felt scrubbed clean, like I never had before. For more than five months, I cried almost everyday, having grown so used to it that when the tears came, I said, "Okay, here you are again. Because of you I am able to heal. Bring it on, sister."

I created alot of s p a c e in my 56th year. My world was rocked to the core, the losses came at me like baseballs from an automated pitching machine. It was an experience that I wouldn't have volunteered for, but it was a necessary one, and I didn't come out unchanged. I was awakened.

As I transition into my 57th birthday on November 18, a new year officially begins. I will spend the entire week celebrating, including a visit to my naturopath, the standing invitation for dinner at my sister and brother-in-law's, and a massage. I will bathe in the phone calls and the birthday cards and the lunches with friends, but most of all I will remember how truly blessed I am.

Now, I am one year stronger inside and, I might add, softer around the edges too. I know that every decision - even the decision to move in with him so quickly - supported my growth and healing. I can actually laugh about it, and I am more compassionate, forgiving, and humble. Today, I feel jazzed, my light is shining bright, and I am once again connected to the vibrant flame of love.

Disappointment is the fastest chariot to enlightenment.

– Buddha

God doesn't give you the people you want,
He gives you the people you NEED ...
to help you, to hurt you, to leave you, to love you
and to make you into the person you were meant to be.

– anonymous

Renew thyself completely each day;
do it again, and again, and forever again.

– Chinese Inscription

TAKING CARE OF YOU

From an early age, many of us (especially women) are programmed to take care of others. We learn to protect their feelings, often at the expense of our own. Sometimes, we are labeled selfish for wanting something or maybe we find ourselves being judged and criticized for what we thought, said, or did. Ultimately, this turned us into passive/ aggressive, unhappy people-pleasers.

Contrary to what we have learned, taking care of ourselves is not selfish; it is about self-love. Being selfish is not about compromising ourselves because compromise leaves us feeling unable to live our lives to the fullest. Therefore, if we don't take care of ourselves first, then everyone around us suffers, including those who need us the most.

Taking care of ourselves also builds self-esteem and gives us a sense of empowerment. Besides the basics - eating three squares, exercising, and practicing good hygiene - taking care of ourselves also includes tending to our mental, emotional, and spiritual health.

Here are twenty-eight ways to help you take better care of yourself:

1. Set clear, firm boundaries around family members, friends, and coworkers who are toxic (i.e., angry, emotionally abusive, negative, and/or stuck on repeat).

2. Say yes to yourself first. If saying no to others is difficult, do it in a way that sounds affirmative and makes you feel good about yourself. For example, say, "I'm not getting a big yes about taking on another commitment right now," or "my intuition is telling me to stay home tonight."

3. The quality of life depends on the choices that we make. Make decisions based on your values and think with the end result in mind.

4. Build a safe, nonjudgmental network of people who will support you through the tough times.

5. Practice verbal kindness towards yourself. Avoid calling yourself stupid, ugly, fat or anything else that you would label abusive if someone else defined you in that way. Keep a picture of yourself as a child, placed where you see it everyday, as a reminder that s/he hears everything you say.

6. Spend time with people who not only love, respect, and appreciate you, but who make you laugh. The average child laughs 140 times a day while the average adult laughs only 4. Laughter generates endorphins that are calming, reduce anxiety, and lower blood pressure.

7. Compulsive thinking is a form of self-badgering. Strive for excellence instead of perfectionism. Anne Lamott warn us that "perfectionism is the voice of the oppressor, the enemy of the people. It will keep you cramped and insane your whole life."

8. Give yourself permission to change your mind.

9. Challenge beliefs that no longer serve you.

10. Honor your limitations.

11. Consume as many "live," whole foods as you can; they are designed to energize, nourish, and restore your body.

12. Maintain a limber body by stretching which releases tension & tightness and creates s p a c e for more energy and lightness to fill your mind and body.

13. Sleep when you are tired; invest in a good mattress and pillow.

14. Wear things that make you feel good about yourself. Avoid shoes that are too tight and clothes that are uncomfortable.

15. Schedule downtime to rebuild reserve.

16. Use some of your sick days at work for wellness days.

17. Give yourself the *s p a c e* to leave a party, event, or family gathering just before you are ready to go.

18. Know when it's time to get professional care. Pain is optional and choosing to suffer is selfish to both you and those around you.

19. Strive to lead with alternative medicine first, which works with, not against, your body's natural ability to heal itself.

20. Create a safe, nurturing environment in which to live. Your soul needs a sanctuary - no matter how small the *s p a c e* - to restore itself.

21. Take care of those possessions that you rely on. For example, if you don't maintain your car and it breaks down causing you stress, this is an indirect way of not taking care of yourself.

22. Avoid spiritual arrogance, i.e., thinking you have it all together or that you are better than others.

23. Trust your intuition, which knows the correct answer if we keep our mind and ego out of the way. Ask yourself questions that require a yes or no answer and phrase them specifically as well as clearly. For added "security", as well as for fun, use a pendulum for guidance.

24. Utilize the breath often, not only to bring you back to the present moment, but to cleanse, energize, and relax you.

25. To neutralize mental clutter, use the following affirmation:

"Even though I _____,

(think, act, feel, say)

I deeply and completely love and accept myself."

26. Begin each day by setting an intention for how you want your day to go. It can be a word, phrase, mantra, symbol or a prayer.

27. Since most of us are not mind readers, ask for what you want. If this feels scary, start by asking for something small. Notice if you are someone who would rather take care of others (by not asking them for anything) than get your needs met.

28. Practice gratitude, the heart's memory. The more you are grateful for, the more that will be given to you. Melody Beattie says, "Gratitude unlocks the fullness of life. It turns what we have into enough, and more. It turns denial into acceptance, chaos to order, confusion to clarity. It can turn a meal into a feast, a house into a home, a stranger into a friend. Gratitude makes sense of our past, brings peace for today, and creates a vision for tomorrow."

Commit yourself to do whatever it is you can contribute in order to create a healthy and sustainable future - the world needs you desperately. Find that in yourself and make a commitment - that is what will change the world.

– John Denver

A sad thing in life is that sometimes
you meet someone who means a lot to you
only to find out in the end that it was never bound to be
and you just have to let go.

– unknown

THE FLOATING OPERA

"People are going to come in and out of your life," Michael reminded me as I chewed the meat off of a baby back rib. Between mouthfuls of tender, succulent pork, I told him about a recent phone call from my friend, Summer*.

I puckered my lip, then imitated the voice of my three-year-old kid inside. "She doesn't want to be my friend anymore."

"Her reason?" Michael asked.

I speared through a chunk of German potato salad.

"She doesn't like my idea of wanting to eliminate Christmas presents this year. You know, my quest to simplify life."

Michael pointed to the teak salad bowl, which I had filled with purple cabbage, walnuts, raisins, blue cheese, and scallions before tossing with a celery seed vinaigrette. Using two wooden salad spoons, I lifted a generous portion onto his plate and went on with my story.

"I told Summer it would be one less gift that she would have to buy."

"And?"

"She told me that it wasn't the point."

Michael pulled off another rib from his rack.

"It's the floating opera, Kater Lynn."

. . . .

Michael and I met through a friend at a party in the mid 1980's. The one thing I remember was that he came through the front door, slipped quietly past the living room, and made a beeline for the kitchen. It was there that he stationed himself for the rest of the evening. And that's where we were introduced, in the kitchen, when I went to refill my glass with Chardonnay.

Wearing a light blue Brooks Brothers shirt and khaki pants, Michael was handsome and tall, with wire rimmed glasses and a thick mop of black hair. I was attracted to intelligent-looking men with dark hair and olive skin, a striking contrast to my fair skinned Wendy Wasp looks.

Despite our obvious physical differences, we found a few things in common - foreign flicks, Italian food, and living alone. Not only did our significant others leave us, but we both alluded to the fact that we weren't ready to jump back into another relationship.

From that night on, our friendship took flight. Michael and I gradually fell into a rhythm of getting together once a week. Since I didn't own a television at the time, we spent most of our time at his place. More often than not, we would get stoned and either go out for dinner or order something in and watch a rented movie.

At the time, I had my own catering business. He was a sales rep for a prestigious tobacco company and traveled during the week. Michael took a genuine interest in my work, encouraging me to take my business to the next level.

He would watch me drive off in my dented black Ford Escort station wagon, which was way past its prime. I had a standard, boring black and white business card. Even the clothes that I wore for client appointments lacked that "dress for success" look.

One evening, we ended up at my place, poured some wine, and held a mini brainstorming session. Michael thought that I needed a new name for my business.

"How about Kater & Company?" he finally suggested, retrieving something from his black leather purse filled with tobacco. "After all, your name is Kater and the servers who come with you can be the 'Company.'"

And, so it was.

At Michael's urging, I hired someone to design a two-color business card on nice white stock. It was striking, one that we both loved. I also invested in a navy blue suit.

Within a year, in 1986, I was catering a $30,000 affair. All of this was orchestrated out of my 400 square foot efficiency apartment with a galley kitchen. From then on, Michael referred to my apartment as "The International World Headquarters of Kater & Company."

One week after this extravagant party, I bought a brand new Subaru station wagon right off the showroom floor. Six weeks later, my new KATERCO license plates arrived in the mail.

"It's all about image, and learning how to play the game in business, Kater Lynn," Michael reminded me.

Michael was the only person who called me by my first and middle name. He told me that the most important word in the English language is someone's name and, salesman or not, he always made an effort to remember a name.

One Friday night, as he was filling the bowl of his favorite Dunhill pipe with Three Nuns tobacco, I told him that one of my clients hired another caterer.

Michael looked up.

"Kater Lynn, it's the floating opera."

"Okay, so what's the floating opera?"

I watched him take the pipe out of his mouth, tamp the tobacco down into its bowl, light it three times, and put it back in his mouth.

"Imagine," he said, talking with the pipe in his mouth, "that you are sitting on the edge of a river. You notice a boat slowly floating into your field of vision. Gradually, it moves closer and closer until it is right in front of you. But, the boat doesn't stop. It keeps floating downstream and out of sight again."

I excused myself to get a second glass of wine from the kitchen.

"Sorry for the interruption...go on," I said, taking a swallow of White Zinfandel.

"People in our lives are like those boats floating down the river. Sometimes we only have a small window of time with them. They come and they go and although we may want to stop or control them, we can't. It is our attachment to them that causes us pain."

I thought about all the wasted mental and emotional s p a c e taken up over my loyalty to people and outcomes and expectations.

He lit his pipe again, using a gold-plated lighter that was given to him by his ex-wife.

"Sometimes, you will chose to let people go, or they may let you go."

He had given me my own pipe and, for a while, I am hooked on the ritual of smoking tobacco. Sometimes in our silence, if a fly were on the wall, we looked like two statues sitting in a fog of smoke.

The phone rang, incurring no reaction on Michael's part.

"If I remember correctly, you were pretty upset by Summer's decision to end the friendship because you didn't want to exchange Christmas gifts. Now, you're upset about losing that catering job. The truth is that unless you have done something hurtful to someone, it's not about you, it's about them."

Michael proceeded to clean out his Dunhill by running a pipe cleaner through the stem. Then he put the pipe back in his mouth to blow out the last remains of tobacco.

I appreciated Michael for his simple, no-nonsense approach to life. He restores my faith in men, some of whom have failed me miserably. We have become buddies without significant others.

"You know," I said to him one day, "when I think back on my life, whenever someone has left me, another person seems to show up. Like the day before my grandmother took her last breath, I witnessed the birth of my first godchild."

. . . .

A couple of years after Michael came into my life, I stopped drinking. Our lives began to slip out of sync, the way two people sometimes do when one of the things that brought them together changes.

Eventually, Michael started dating his acupuncturist and I met my future husband, Terry. Still, Michael and I would catch up occasionally, just like old times. One night, over chicken fajitas, he told me that he was moving to Little Rock.

"My company is luring me with more money. I wanted to tell you in person."

I put my fork down and remembered the floating opera. I thought about how generous Michael had been and how he had helped me turn my catering business around. I valued his perspective and appreciated what he taught me about life and relationships and kindness.

"God, Michael, are you really leaving?"

. . . .

Six weeks later, after he bought my sofa bed and I threw him a surprise going-away party, he moved to Arkansas.

For a while, he stayed in touch by phone while I fed his "smile pile" - a collection of letters, postcards, photographs, and cartoons that he collected from his friends and family over the years.

"I really appreciate everything that you send me," Michael told me over the phone.

· · · · · · · ·

One year after living in Little Rock, Michael called to tell me that his kidney was showing signs of distress.

"You're kidding," I responded, not knowing what else to say.

"Saul is going to donate one of his kidneys."

Saul, a gifted chiropractor and free spirit type who wears a small hoop in his right ear, is Michael's kid brother.

"Well, there's the blessing, Michael," I said.

"He's moving from New Mexico to come and live with me. We can take care of each other. Saul's recovery will be much longer than mine, you know."

I didn't know that the donor had a lengthier, more painful recovery. Even so, I felt better knowing that Michael wasn't going to go through this alone. What little family he had was scattered all over the country.

After we hung up, I filled the washing machine with towels, wiped fingerprints from the walls, and went through the mail. One of my best defenses against sadness is to get busy.

· · · · · · · ·

A few weeks later, Saul moved in with Michael and the kidney transplant was a success. After recuperating for a couple of months, Michael told me that he had never felt better. His job at the prestigious tobacco company was waiting for him and Saul was moving back to New Mexico.

Gradually, over the next two years, my conversations with Michael tapered off to once a month, then every time the seasons changed. I began to notice that he was becoming more self-centered, dominating our phone conversations with talk about himself and his life in Little Rock. If he called first, it took me longer to get back to him.

On my fiftieth birthday, Michael called to tell me that his kidney was failing again.

"It could last for two, three, maybe four years. At this point, the doctor can't predict. When he mentioned dialysis, I told him that it wasn't an option, period."

"You'll die, Michael."

"Maybe," he said, sounding annoyed. "My doctor was able to help me get on disability. I'm going to stay where I am, take some time off from work, and figure out what I want to do with the rest of my life."

I was angry and told him so. For years, Michael complained about how people on disability were sucking the financial marrow out of our country.

His response was predictable.

"Life goes on, Kater Lynn."

He had also forgotten to wish me a happy birthday.

. . . .

Four months after 9/11, I woke up with a spiritual urge to go and see Michael in Little Rock. When Terry opened his eyes, I told him about it.

"When do you want to go?" he asked.

"Soon."

That day, I decided to call Michael, who sounded somewhat surprised by my decision. He told me that, except for his brother Saul, no one had come to visit him in Arkansas. I decided not to tell him about my spiritual urge.

The night before my trip, I packed my suitcase. At the last minute, I decided to take one of my photo albums. I also threw in some photographs of my fiftieth birthday party, along with an old snapshot of Michael sitting in a navy blue captain's chair taken at "The International World Headquarters of Kater & Company."

The next day, on a cold Monday morning in January, my flight took off nonstop from Baltimore to Little Rock. Still shaken from 9/11, the cabin wasn't even half full. I passed time by gazing out the window and flipping through the airline magazine. In one article, I read that "salvation lies in remembering."

Two hours and forty minutes later, the wheels on the plane hit the ground at Little Rock National Airport. When it finally stopped at the gate, I unbuckled my seat belt and hoisted a forest green backpack over my shoulder. In a couple of days, I would be returning home.

Once in the terminal, I followed the signs to baggage claim where I spotted Michael from a distance. He looked the same except that his Beatles-mop hairstyle was even thicker and longer than I remembered. It almost looked like he was wearing a motorcycle helmet on his head.

"Kater Lynn," he said in his usual reserved way as I approached him.

"Well, I remembered to bring everything but my sunglasses."

"No problem," he assured me, "I've got a spare in the car."

With that, we were off to retrieve my suitcase. It was 10:00 a.m. when we left the airport and drove through downtown Little Rock en route to his apartment. Knowing that I had never been to this part of the country, Michael took it upon himself to be my tour guide.

"Arkansas is considered the buckle on the Bible belt," he informed me. "There are approximately two million people in the state. When deer season opens, 300,000 people show up."

I rolled my eyes.

"Less than 1% of the population makes over $50,000 a year."

Then he proceeded to tell me about the people and how friendly they are and that life's pace is very slow.

"Here in this part of the world you might be standing in line at the grocery store and a customer is taking pictures out of their wallet to show the cashier. No one seems to mind. You just talk to the person in front or back of you until they're finished."

The terrain in this part of Arkansas was hillier than I had imagined. I rummaged through my backpack for some Chapstick.

"Back east, people are different. They're not as friendly," he said. "You go into a convenience store and give them money and they don't even say hello."

I told Michael, in an attempt to change the subject, that Little Rock sounds like the perfect place for him. He didn't take the bait.

So, I listened patiently while he force-fed the virtues of Arkansas down my throat. When I found a s p a c e in the conversation to insert a thought, I pointed out that he was talking generalities.

"People are merely a reflection of our attitude," I reminded him defensively. "It's rare that I say hello to someone that they don't say hello back."

My first internal button is pushed as we drive up the hill to his apartment complex. It's not even lunchtime and, already, I want to turn around and go home.

Michael lives in a high rise that was constructed in the 1950's. Even though it looks dated, the outside is quite charming. He doesn't have a view of downtown Little Rock, but the occupants in the next building do.

He pointed to the building that has the view of the skyline.

"I'm on a waiting list to get a one bedroom apartment in that building."

After we got out of the car, he rolled my Hartman through the lobby and into the vintage elevator. It was a very slow ride to the sixth floor.

His apartment was to the right of the elevator. Once he inserted the key and opened the door, I immediately moved down the long hallway and into his living room to the bookshelves that I remembered from his apartment in Baltimore.

I propped my suitcase against the wall and took a closer look. Only the things that were familiar stood out - several cans of McClelland "Dark Star" tobacco, the picture of his ex-wife, an origami pipe that I had given him, three model antique cars, and a humidor.

He saw me looking at the humidor.

"When you gave that to me, you forgot to take the price tag off, Kater Lynn. Do you remember that?"

"Not really."

I picked it up, turned it over and, sure enough, the $40.00 price tag was still there.

I put it back and began to scan the room. On one wall was the picture of him dancing with his late mother, whom he adored. Assorted crystals and stones lined the windowsill behind a leather easy chair. He walked over and pointed to the piece of rock salt that I had brought back with me from The Dead Sea.

My eyes continued to move around the living room. He still had the camel saddle that his brother Saul had given him from Tehran, along with the sofa bed that he had bought from me. Finally, I circled around to the bookshelves where I spotted one of my all-time favorite books, *The Seed*. Secretly, I wished I hadn't given it to him because it was out of print.

"When I knew you were coming," Michael said, "I went through my smile pile and pulled a few pictures and some cards. I also found a couple of photographs that you gave me."

"Let's go through them later," I said.

When I picked up my suitcase, he showed me to his office where I would be sleeping for the next two nights. There was no sofa bed, sleeping bag, or cot in sight.

Sensing my concern, he reassured me that he had a blowup mattress in the closet.

Then I followed him into the bathroom where he pointed out my towels. On the way back to the living room, I grabbed the photo album from my suitcase. It was a little 4" x 6" theme album about Sweet Potato. Michael loved Sweet Potato and always asked about her when we talked on the phone.

He sat at the dining room table with the album while I read a magazine. From the corner of my eye, I could see that he was flipping through it very quickly. Obviously, he wasn't reading anything that I wrote. Even though this was my problem, I still felt agitated.

He closed the album and got up from the table, making no comment about it.

I asked him if he had received the story that I sent him about my trip to Paris.

"Yeah, it's in the pile with the rest of your stories."

Just as I am thinking that he might be holding some sort of resentment, he asked me what I wanted to do for lunch.

"Let's go out," I suggested, already thinking that a change of scenery would be good for both of us.

"Okay, Kater Lynn."

While he moved at a snail's pace to gather his tobacco paraphernalia, I pushed buttons on the television remote.

Finally, we grabbed our coats, rode the elevator, and walked around the apartment complex. He wanted to show me the walkways and the patio overlooking the swimming pool. Except for the dull roar of a busy road nearby, the place was beautiful. After we went all the way around on foot, we got in the car and drove back down the hill to the land of deer hunters and Bible thumpers.

"I heard that there is great barbecue in this part of the country."

"Ahhh...I know just where to take you. It's only the best in Little Rock."

The best in Little Rock turned out to be pretty pedestrian. I opted for pork instead of chicken or beef, which came piled high on a white bun with some coleslaw on the side. Even though it went down like a charm, I knew that it was the wrong octane for my fuel tank. I would need to take a nap, so after lunch we left and headed back to his apartment. Then, for lack of motivation on both of our parts, we ended up there for the rest of the day.

. . . .

On Tuesday morning, I woke up early, grabbed my cell phone, and took the elevator to the ground floor to call Terry.

I told him that Michael was bringing out the worst in me, that I was feeling defensive and totally invested in being right. I also told him that I knew that this was my reaction to Michael's ardent opinions and self-righteous behavior.

I started to cry.

"I know that the easy thing to do would be to give him some excuse that I have to leave early, but my conscience won't allow me to do it. Besides, deep down, I know that there's a reason for me to be here."

"That's my wife," Terry said.

For the next two days, my time with Michael was strung together with errands, meals, watching television, and talking. However, unlike the old days, we weren't as comfortable in our silence.

On Wednesday morning, I woke up early again and ambled into the living room. I was guided to pickup *The Seed*, the spiritual book that I had given Michael several years ago. With my eyes closed, I opened it randomly because, in my state of mind, any page would do. The message was, of course, perfect. Since the thin paperback was out of print, I decided to get it photocopied before my flight home later that afternoon.

Michael woke up and we spent our last day together, much like the other two. After his morning errands, we ate lunch at a family-owned Greek restaurant. He and I both ordered a grilled pita filled with homemade falafel, lettuce, tomatoes, feta, and tahini sauce. The combination of colors, flavors, and textures was to die for.

"Hey, Michael," I suggested between mouthfuls, "let's not forget to go through the things that you pulled from your smile pile when we get back to the apartment."

"Okay, Kater Lynn."

While he paid the check, I checked my airline ticket again to see what time my flight was leaving. On the way back to the apartment, we headed over to the office supply store where I photocopied *The Seed* to take home with me.

As we drove up the hill to his apartment complex for the last time, he asked me if I wanted to stop at the local smoke shop on the way to the airport.

"We can go if you want," I said, reluctantly.

"It's the only one in Little Rock."

Michael talked a lot about the guys at the smoke shop and how much time he spends there.

 Once inside the apartment again, he grabbed the stuff from his smile pile, sat on the sofa, and started handing me things - one at a time. First, a picture of me at a Grateful Dead concert in Telluride, Colorado. Then, a cartoon that I had sent him of a man smoking a pipe walking his dog who is smoking a pipe. Next, he handed me a Kater & Company business card.

I got up to go to the bathroom. When I returned, he passed me a birthday card with a parrot on the front. Inside, in calligraphy, I had written: Life really does begin at 40, so...enjoy the flight. It was signed "Always your friend, Kater."

Together, we laughed and reminisced and, for a short while, it felt like old times. As he got up to put his smile pile stack back in the shoebox, I realized that whatever had been bugging each of us these last two days had appeared to work itself out.

I looked at the clock and told him that it was time to go. We gathered my stuff and drove down the steep hill toward the smoke shop located in a strip shopping center on the other side of town.

When we got there, I followed Michael into the store. There, clustered around a table was an assortment of chairs - wooden chairs, lawn chairs, captain's chairs, folding chairs - were men with yellowish brown stained teeth who greeted him by name. This was the hub of the store, a gathering place for men of all ages to smoke their tobacco and share stories.

After Michael introduced me to everyone, I made my way over to the humidor. While I have little interest in cigars, I have always been curious about humidors. Humidors are containers, cabinets or, in this case, rooms with circulation fans and humidifiers that ensure the proper humidity distribution for the purpose of aging cigars.

Humidors are not only a feast for the senses, but quiet - away from all the smoke and idle chatter in the shop. I found it fascinating to look at the thousands of cigars from all over the world lined up perfectly in their own special boxes. I picked one up. The outside of the cigar felt slightly brittle to the touch and smelled like burned dirt.

As I turned to leave the humidor and walk around the store, Michael approached me.

"On Saturday afternoons, there are so many people that come here to hang out that they have to bring their own chairs. Sometimes I come in at 1:00 and don't leave until 5:00."

"I can understand why you like this place," I said, a hint of compassion in my voice.

Clearly, Michael was in his element here. After browsing around for a while longer, I motioned for him to meet me outside. The smell of cigar smoke was giving me a headache.

He followed me out.

"It's too bad that you didn't spend more time with the guys," he said as we crossed the parking lot to the car.

"I can't handle the smell of smoke anymore."

On the way to the airport, we stopped for gas. While Michael went inside the convenience store to pay for it, I grabbed my photocopy of *The Seed* and reread the passage from earlier that morning:

> *We outgrow people, places, and things as we unfold. We may be saddened when old friends say their peace and leave our lives...but let them go. They were at a different stage...looking in a different direction. They stood still while you advanced in your thoughts and aspirations and the friendship was strained for a long time, but neither party had the heart to let it go. Remember we have no duty to drag them along with us as we grow. There is nothing to give each other any more...and one day you see a stranger behind the other's eyes, eyes you once thought you knew.*

When Michael returned to the car, he loaded his pipe, stuffing the tobacco into the bowl with his index finger. Then he lit it three times, tamped it down, and lit it again. In all the years that I have known him, this routine has never changed.

Finally, we arrived at Little Rock National Airport. At the curb, we gave each other a hug. He said that it was great to see me and I, in turn, thanked him for his hospitality. Then, as he drove off in what he called his white "mommy" van, I - without looking back - ducked into the terminal for my flight home.

*After a five-year hiatus, Summer and I reconnected over coffee and scones. She agreed that being disgruntled wasn't about my wanting to simplify my life. As it turned out, I had unknowingly inflicted an emotional wound on her. By her shining some light on it, we were able to clear things up, deepen our friendship, and move forward.

*Bless everyone for being a part of your life,
whether they came for a reason, a season, or a lifetime.*

– unknown

*Time is God's way of not allowing
everything to happen all at once.*

— unknown

TIME

Perhaps the most elusive thing in our lives, and one of the biggest challenges that we face today, is the issue of time. We just don't seem to have enough of it. Time is the beast that can't be tamed. It is fixed and unvarying and, because we define it in concrete terms, our lives revolve around calendars, deadlines, and clocks.

Time has been, and always will be, one of the core mysteries of human life. These days, the feeling of time closing in on us creates more and more stress. Stress drives us to multitask. And, when we are multitasking, we are never doing any one thing very well, nor are we fully engaged in living either.

One would think that the combination of high speed Internet, "on demand" television, and nanotechnology would give us more time, but it doesn't. All they seem to do is give us the ability to cram more in. Other distractions include the abundance of information, choices, options, and activities. While they have benefits, they fill up our time and leave us little room to process our thoughts, behaviors, and feelings. No wonder 24 hours rarely seems like enough.

To create more *s p a c e* for time, I am not talking about time management where we follow a strict code of ethics to gain more control. It's more about priority management, a lifestyle change where you strike a balance between the *have to's* and the *want to's*.

A *have to* list are things like handling the mail, paying bills and grocery shopping. It might include exercise. Of course, this doesn't include the unexpected things like a car repair, medical emergency, or a family crisis.

The *want to's* are things that bring meaning to your life, give you a sense of purpose, and make you feel good. These things are sacred, and you are the only one who can protect them.

Want to's and *have to's* can also be the same. One example might be your work. You love what you do, but you also have to make a living. Taking care of yourself could also fall under both categories. So does caring for your children.

The thing about time is that if you don't find time for yourself, then you won't get it. It's okay to be selfish with your time because time is what makes up your life. Personally, I don't like to waste time gossiping on the phone, spending time with people who drain my energy, or participate in activities that take me away from what is important. People who understand this are also selfish with their time, too.

Here are twenty-two ways to expand the *s p a c e* for more time in your life:

1. Avoid wasting time by saying "I'll try." Trying is lying; you're either doing it or you aren't. Saying that you don't have time is an overused, convenient excuse to avoid the truth which is that what you are being asked to do isn't a priority.

2. Begin to notice who the "time thieves" are. They might include spending time with people who siphon your energy or add nothing to your life. They could also be your children or significant other who lean on you to do things that they could do for themselves (for solutions, see *Life with Kids*).

3. To deepen your relationship with time, avoid procrastination which robs time and personal pleasure. Set boundaries if you have the dreaded disease to please. Begin to look at things that you do out of a self-imposed obligation. Take the word "should" out of your vocabulary.

4. Hire someone to do what you don't like to do so that you can do what you want. If money is an issue, consider sacrificing one restaurant meal a week in exchange for having

someone come and clean your house or watch your kids for three hours. At the very least, this may give you a sense of having more time for yourself.

5. Protect yourself from professional people who don't value your time. For example, ask to be your doctor's first appointment of the day. Another option is to call first to see if he or she is running on time, or ask them to call you. We must teach people to respect our time.

6. It takes time to nurture and maintain relationships. Choose wisely the people with whom you spend time.

7. Keep an ongoing grocery list on your refrigerator. Every time you run out of something, write it down. That way, not only will you have a head start on your grocery shopping, but the likelihood of multiple trips or overspending is minimized – another time saver.

8. Eating out is more time consuming than staying home if you prepare easy whole food meals (see *Detox Your Kitchen*).

9. Whether you cook for four or fourteen, the amount of work is almost the same. You still have to plan, shop, prepare, cook, and serve, so you might as well make enough for the next day, or freeze some for later.

10. Time is an expensive commodity. When shopping, make sure you absolutely love what you buy. Having to return something is a time robber.

11. Write things down like reminders and appointments. Plan ahead by combining errands.

12. Apply for an EZ pass, speed pass for gasoline, direct deposit, automatic debit, or anything else that saves you time. It takes time to set them up, but it will save you time down the road.

13. Clutter robs efficiency. Having to find things because you are disorganized steals time. If necessary, hire a professional

organizer, not only to help get your life in order, but to learn how to maintain it.

14. Take care of things in the present moment. For example, when someone wants to get together (assuming that is what you want to do), set up a time then. The same goes for paper. For each piece of paper that crosses your path, either act on it, file it, or throw it out. This takes minutes, while piles take hours.

15. When possible, utilize your most energetic times of day for the things that are most important to you. For most people, this is the morning. One study found that 75% of people who exercise in the morning stick with their programs, while only 25% do if they exercise in the evening.

16. Guard your health; sickness and everything associated with it is time consuming.

17. Reduce phone tag by letting the other person know when they can call you back. When calling a company, wait until you hear "if you are on a rotary phone, please stay on the line." Since most people don't have a rotary phone these days, you may be connected to a live person faster.

18. Go right to the top person in a company if you need a problem resolved. Rather than lead with your complaint, say, "I need your help." These four simple words evoke a sympathetic attitude and usually yield positive results.

19. Saying no to requests for your time can feel like deprivation. Replace no with a more abundant sounding phrase like "my plate is full right now" or "I want to stay focused on what I am doing and, if I say yes, it will take me in another direction." Remember, when we can't say no, we end up overcommitting and underproducing.

20. Nothing that you do, include doing nothing, is wasted time as long as you are enjoying it. Spend time being and/or doing things that nourish your soul. If you like to putter,

practice "senseless acts of beauty" around your house - buy fresh flowers, pitch stuff, change the photographs in your frames, and rearrange things.

21. Having too much time on your hands can be as stressful as not having enough. Turn off the television or computer and get moving. You are not too old to make a difference in the life of someone else. Be a mentor, take a class that challenges your mind, volunteer, or offer to walk a dog that is housebound all day. You'll feel better about yourself and your body will appreciate the exercise.

22. Practice mindfulness by giving tasks your full attention. Slow down and just let yourself be present with it. To keep yourself anchored, connect to your five senses, or focus on the breath. It is in the present moment that we are most connected to the Divine.

*The clock is a conspiracy and
a crime against humanity and
I would not own one
except I miss appointments without it.*

— Brian Andreas

There is no spiritual design for clutter.

— unknown

TOLERATIONS

"You know," my husband said to me one evening after dinner, "living with that slow leak in your tire is a toleration."

I felt slammed against the end of a very long day.

"What are you talking about?" I asked him defensively.

"Tolerations are things in your life that suck energy from you on a regular basis."

"Go on," I said, leafing mindlessly through a pile of mail.

"Putting air in that car tire is something that you have to keep doing until you decide to get it fixed."

Hmmm. . . I thought to myself.

The next day, after he left for work, I flipped through the dictionary to see how *Websters* defines toleration. After scanning through four different meanings, I picked the one that resonated the most: "To put up with."

Clearly, I was putting up with that leak in my tire and it was really stressing me out.

Even though everyone's list of tolerations is different, they all share one common thread - they deplete our energy, time, and peace of mind. Eventually, to put up with creates feelings of frustration, anger, resentment, complacency, and feeling out of control.

I decided to make a toleration list for each room in my house. While I didn't have to eliminate all of them right away, at least it motivated me to get started. I began to tackle the room where I spent the most time - the kitchen (you can also choose the room that is causing you the most stress). Then, I committed to release at least one toleration a week.

Some of the tolerations on my list included sharpening a dull kitchen knife, replacing a missing knob on a drawer, changing a light bulb, tossing out pens that didn't work, staging things where I would use them, and replacing a lousy can opener with a more functional one.

No toleration is insignificant. Sometimes, they are so subtle that we don't even realize the impact that they have on our sense of well-being. I also discovered that the easiest ones to let go of often move the most energy.

Granted, some tolerations will require more effort, patience, and time. Let's face it; sewing a missing button on my favorite sweater (so that I could finally wear it after two years) is very different from changing how I react when Terry plops his briefcase in the middle of the kitchen counter.

Then there will be tolerations that you have little or no control over such as chronic pain, living with an inconsiderate neighbor, or having to care for a terminally ill family member. These will need to be modified, meaning that in order to change the situation, you will have to change.

The more tolerations you get rid of, the less you will be able to tolerate in your life. Other tolerations that I have eliminated include noisy places, eating bad tasting food, clutter, shoes that look good but hurt my feet, retail stores that don't value my business, cigarette smoke, being around angry and/ or controlling people, local television news, and violent movies. While my list has shrunk considerably over the years, tolerations remain ongoing for the simple reason that life happens - things break, issues surface, and change is inevitable.

After a while, you will begin to notice that reducing tolerations will simplify your life. Every time something is modified, eliminated, or accepted, you will feel motivated, energized, and lighter. It will also save precious time, reduce stress, and give you a sense of accomplishment.

Soon after my car tire was fixed, I stopped by Terry's office to photocopy something. On the wall, I noticed an 11" x 17" color poster from Coach University Press. Printed across the middle in rather large, lower case letters were two words - "tolerate nothing." The remaining *s p a c e* was filled with line after line of toleration examples:

Kids bursting into the bathroom without knocking

Customers whose checks bounce

A windowless office

A slow draining bathroom sink

Dull scissors

The dog getting into the trash

A kitten shredding the sofa (but she is so cute)

Lower back problems from sitting in a bad chair all day

Chewing fingernails to the quick

Feeling pressured to call family

Feeling depressed and not taking action

A snoring spouse

Being around negative people

Over planning

A flickering computer screen

Sugar addiction

Not adopting and sticking to project time lines

A bad driver's license picture

Children complaining when they are asked to help

Fear of being assertive at work

Being manipulated with guilt

Needing bifocals

Dwelling on sadness about life's disappointments

Saying yes when no is a better choice

The list was endless.

As I was preparing to leave his office that day, I found myself rummaging through my pocketbook for the car keys. The shoulder bag was way too small for the amount of stuff I needed to carry. I had outgrown the color, it didn't have any compartments, and I was tired of digging. Clearly, a new, more functional handbag would eliminate another toleration in my life...

Inch by inch is a cinch. Yard by yard is hard.

– unknown

The most courageous thing a person can do
is to live an authentic life. What is an authentic life?
It is a life lived from your heart, speaking the truth,
standing in your truth, living in your truth.

– Terri Amos

TRUTH

January 2, 2005. Today, my life is going to change. It isn't that I am giving up refined sugar, vowing to spend more time on my yoga mat, or resolving to finish this book. It goes much deeper, something that I am definitely not prepared for.

The day before, on New Year's Day, Terry woke up, worked out at the gym, and returned home in a foul mood. Something about our next door neighbor, he told me. I decided to leave him alone and, as the morning progressed, his mood softened. This, I will guess, was the result of him finally deciding to tackle six months worth of unopened mail.

From the other room, I could hear the sounds of ripping and tearing while The Tournament of Roses Parade was on television. To help him with this daunting task (he would rather stick needles in his eye), I made him a little "coupon" book for Christmas. In it, he could redeem the coupons for a pedicure, a meatloaf dinner, a trip to the local ice cream store, and help with his mail. I had it all figured out. Each day, I would open the mail, pitch the junk, and put the rest in the bathroom drawer next to the toilet.

The next day, on January 2 - the morning of the day that would change my life - we were in the process of trying to get out of the house to visit my brother and *sister-in-law. Feeling rushed, I asked Terry to prepare the food for our two dogs. While I finished something on the computer, I heard him fumbling with something in the kitchen.

"What's going on out there?" I asked, peeking around the corner from my office.

"This plastic wrap is useless," he shot back, proceeding to rip the edge of the box.

Now, I don't like having things ripped apart and told him to get some tape and fix it. He didn't like having me tell him what to do and proceeded to throw the box across the kitchen floor.

"What is wrong with you?" I yelled.

And that's when my life changed.

"I don't want to be married to you anymore," he said.

. . . .

Terry and I first laid eyes on each other at an Insight Seminar, one of several personal growth organizations that sprung up in the nineteen eighties. Midway through the intensive five-day seminar, he confessed to a mutual friend that if his instincts were right, I was going to be his wife. That was on October 11, 1989. Three years later to the day, we were married next to the lapping waters of the Chesapeake Bay underneath the canopy of a full moon.

At the time, we were wildly infatuated by a mutual desire to heal old wounds and feel whole again. It would be the same reason that made him decide to transition out of our marriage.

"I'm not growing in this relationship anymore," Terry confessed, picking up the roll of plastic wrap that had fallen out of the broken box.

During our courtship and throughout the marriage, we sought couple's counseling from time to time. Blending eighty years of history often requires professional help, mostly to deal with the scratchy aspects of living with another human being. To add to our laundry list of challenges, we were exact opposites. I am an introverted self-learner, brunette, a neatnik, right-handed, a Deadhead, and yogini. He is an extrovert, a perpetual student, a red head, a clutter bug, a southpaw, a symphony goer, and a sailor. While I am happy to stay at home, he wants to venture

Terry and I on our wedding day.
October 11, 1992

out and explore. But what made it work for us was a foundation of mutual respect, trust, friendship…and our commitment to personal growth.

Sometime in the seventh year of our marriage, I was ready for a deeper connection with Terry. We agreed to another round of marriage counseling, but after several sessions, it was evident that the breakthrough I was looking for wasn't going to happen. So, I decided to let go of how I thought the marriage should be and accept it for what it was. After all, our life together was pretty good and I was, by all accounts, content.

"Our relationship has become one of convenience for both of us," he said, taping the plastic wrap box back together.

Yes, we took very good care of each other. While he went out in the world to hunt and gather, I was more than happy to keep the home fires burning. He paid the bills and I balanced the checkbook. We did for each other what the other didn't want to do and, as Joni Mitchell wrote, "it was a warm arrangement."

"I've known it for a long time, that our relationship is one of convenience," Terry said, pausing, "and you know it, too."

Then he left me standing there with the truth.

"Give me a couple of minutes and I'll be ready," I told him in a mild state of shock.

I probably brushed my teeth, turned off the computer, and grabbed a few things from the kitchen counter for the ride to visit my brother, sister-in-law, and their two boys.

As we drove in silence, my mind jumped from one thought to another in an attempt to make sense of it all. Yes, Terry had seemed unusually moody and irritable in the last few months. The week before Christmas, when I innocently forgot to turn off my cell phone at The Baltimore Country Club, his face got so red that I thought he was going to burst a blood vessel. His reaction was most interesting, especially since it took him five years to get me to agree to even own a cell phone, much less remember to keep it turned on.

The next day, he confessed that his trigger reaction was a result of some unresolved "preverbal" stuff from his childhood that he was working on with his therapist.

Okay, I thought.

Now, as his new champagne-colored Subaru Outback crossed over the Chesapeake Bay Bridge toward Easton where my brother and his family live, a wide spectrum of fears surfaced. I felt vulnerable and exposed and scared of the unknown.

A wave of shame came over me that the secret was out about us, that we were no longer the happy couple that everyone perceived us to be. But mostly, I felt sad at the thought of losing my partner of twelve years, not counting the three before we were married.

When we turned down the street where my brother lived, I told him I couldn't believe this was happening.

"Yeah, I know," he said, an air of sad surrender in his voice.

I managed to make it through the afternoon with my family. Even though my life was falling apart, I wore the mask of a happy face, just like I had learned to do as a kid.

That night, my sleep pattern rollercoasted its way through the alpha, beta, and delta states. When my eyes opened the next morning, Terry was staring out of our bedroom window facing east. The view was spectacular, the newborn sun lifting itself from the horizon of the Chesapeake Bay.

"When I was ten years old," he said, "I promised myself that I would never get a divorce."

Terry's childhood was one of financial privilege and emotional poverty. The eldest son and third in line of four children, he was raised by a handful of nannies who, once Terry became attached to them, were fired by his unreasonable, alcoholic mother. At the age of five, his parents split up. Each parent would remarry and divorce again, ushering in a small flock of half and step siblings.

I got out of bed and before getting dressed rinsed my face, brushed my teeth, and gargled. Then I brushed my hair on the way to the walk-in closet where our eyes met for the first time that morning. There, we put our arms around each other and burst into tears.

"My heart hasn't hurt this much in a long time," Terry said. "I don't know where to go with all of this. We love each other, but I can't put my finger on what is missing in our relationship."

"I can tell you what's missing, honey. We talked about this in therapy four years ago. There's no romance."

A few years back, through an energy healer, we were informed that our souls carried a brother/sister pattern from numerous, previous lifetimes. For one thing, we bickered like siblings often do. Our relationship had a competitive undertone. We were roommates living parallel lives. And, there was no jealousy, even though we each had a stable of crushes on the opposite sex and shared them openly. All of this aside, it was obvious that we were also deeply connected on a soul level.

I threw on my gray sweat pants and a white turtleneck.

"You know," I said to him, "we must both be ready for romance or this wouldn't be showing up in our lives now."

Our work in therapy had focused on how to bring us together as a couple, but the odds seemed stacked against us. After we were married, I kept my maiden name. He sent New Year's cards to his friends; I sent Christmas cards to mine. About half the time, we traveled separately. In an unconscious attempt to bring us closer together, on our tenth anniversary, we finally bought matching wedding bands. Still, with all of our efforts, it didn't ignite the spark.

I opened my top dresser drawer to get a pair of socks.

"For a long time, the relationship worked for us," I said.

He looked at me. "It looks like now it has gone as far as it can go."

Emotionally, the next couple of days were extremely painful, yet heart cleansing at the same time. Terry felt the most emotional in the morning. I, at night. True to form, we remained complementary opposites.

On Thursday night, four days after our decision to separate, we got into bed, turned off the lights, and talked for a while. I told Terry that it will be interesting to think about who I want to tell first and why."

"I've already told Brian," he informed me.

Brian is an old college buddy from Babson and Terry's closest and most trusted friend. Once a month, they meet in Princeton, New Jersey, halfway between Maryland and Connecticut, where he and Brian live, respectively. There, they walk around Palmer Square, catch the crew races, and eat lunch at The Nassau Inn. Then, three or so hours later, they go their separate ways again.

"I haven't told anyone yet," I said to Terry, feeling that all too familiar competitive edge.

The truth is that I wasn't ready to. Disclosure becomes public property, leaves me feeling vulnerable, and opens the door to interpretation. And, that is something I have no control over. But, I must also remember that what other people think is none of my business.

However I will, in an attempt to take care of myself, make sure that the first few people I tell won't dispense unsolicited advice, offer opinions, or make a judgment about my decision. They may or may not include members of my family. They may or may not be my closest friends either. There are some people whom I will want to tell in person because I don't want them to hear it from anyone else. And then there is the person who is going to be the hardest to tell - my mother.

I turned on the ceiling fan, got back into bed, inserted my earplugs, and grabbed my eye pillow from the drawer next to our bed.

. . . .

The following Sunday, one week after we decided to part ways, I was ready to tell my family. My brother who lived on the eastern shore of Maryland and my sister in California would hear the news over the phone. We packed the car with water, snacks, and both dogs before venturing out, household by household. Everyone met the news with shock, sadness, and a willingness to support. Everyone was clear that they wanted to maintain their relationship with Terry.

"I'm so glad this day is behind me," I said to my comrade in arms when we finally coasted down our driveway and into the darkness of the carport.

As the days of those first two weeks blended, one into the other, our friendship deepened. We did things we hadn't done in eons, like go to the movies, hang out on the sofa, and take early morning walks. All served to lighten the emotional load and, by the end of the second week, I couldn't deny that a miracle had happened. Gone was our need to control each other, my having to harp on him, and his underlying current of anger towards me.

"Thanks for your courage to get the ball rolling," I said to him over dinner one evening.

. . . .

Children who grow up in homes where authenticity is valued are seldom afraid or embarrassed to speak their truth. But if you were punished or confronted for feeling a certain way, saying something "inappropriate," or acting from your intuition, it could have easily translated into rejection, abandonment, and/or shame.

The inability to be who we are comes from our parents wanting us to be a reflection of them, society wanting to mold us, and us wanting to fit in with our peers. We end up compromising our own unique characteristics, passions, and behaviors because being authentic was met with indifference. And, since our early survival depended on pleasing others, we learned how to lie, withhold information, and manipulate the truth. Eventually, we have to leave the expectations of others behind and live the way we feel most worthwhile.

I was afraid to confront the failure of my marriage for fear of being abandoned. However, once Terry and I faced the truth, the struggle was over. We agreed that he would stay in the house and I would go. Instead of trying to mentally figure it out, we would "live" it out, allowing our intuitions to dictate the process. To restore balance to our lives, we would also take it one decision at a time, and seek couple's counseling to help us through the transition.

We had come together for the purpose of healing, and our decision to separate was dictated by our souls. I knew that what didn't get resolved in this lifetime was just going to roll over into the next one.

It was evident that our "work" together was done.

* Terry fell in love with my former sister-in-law (who was married to my older brother).

Never apologize for showing feeling.
When you do so, you apologize for truth.

— Benjamin Disraeli

Rarely have we seen a person fail
who has thoroughly followed our path.
Those who do not recover are those who cannot
or will not give themselves completely
to this simple program,
usually men and women who are
constitutionally incapable of being honest
with themselves. There are such unfortunates.
They are not at fault;
they seem to have been born that way.

– From the *A.A. Big Book*

TWELVE GUIDELINES

(to de-cluttering your life)

1. Acknowledge that the root cause of stress comes from clutter whether it is mental, emotional, verbal, visual, material and/or physical.

2. Begin to take an inventory of all the clutter in your life.

3. Make a decision to accept full responsibility for it.

4. Become willing to identify your fears and then choose to move through them.

5. Come to understand and accept that your trigger reactions are opportunities for healing.

6. Ask for support and guidance in your efforts to reduce clutter.

7. Practice patience, flexibility and forgiveness with yourself, remembering that it takes years to accumulate clutter.

8. Make amends to those that you have harmed to lighten your emotional, mental and physical load.

9. Break it down, remain focused and take it one task at a time.

10. Adopt the one in, one out guideline when buying things.

11. Strive to maintain balance by periodically purging anything that no longer serves you.

12. Learn to trust that eliminating clutter attracts the *s p a c e* for something new, better, and/or different to come into your life.

God gives me exactly what I can handle.
I just wish he didn't trust me so much.

– Mother Teresa

How beautiful it is to do nothing,
and then rest afterward.

– Spanish Proverb

VACATION AT HOME

With air travel bordering on insanity, unpredictable gas prices, and stress becoming a national epidemic, why not think about taking your next vacation at home? If your last few getaways included unbearable traffic, long waits in restaurants, and crowded tourist attractions, maybe a "staycation" is for you.

With a little planning, an open mind, and a desire to simplify your life, you can still feel pampered, have fun, and relax. It might be much less stressful, especially if you don't have piles of laundry, e-mail, and phone calls to come home to. And, it's a much gentler way to transition back into your life, work and/or school.

Granted, depending upon your circumstances, preference, and personality, vacationing at home is not for everyone. Most likely, it's not a good fit if the only way you can unwind is to leave town. It probably wouldn't work if you are constantly being reminded of all that has to be done around the house. And, it's not for people who like traveling from place to place, packing & unpacking, sleeping in a different hotel room every night, and sightseeing.

If, on the other hand, you enjoy cruises, resort hotels, spas, visiting out of town friends and relatives, and/or RV camping (with a car in tow), then you probably like to stay in one place and, from there, have the option to come and go - just like you would if you stayed at home. If this sounds like your style, here are some ways to create a relaxing, enjoyable, fun vacation at home:

1. Involve the entire family in the decision-making process. Brainstorm by sharing ideas, interests, and options. When tastes differ, compromise, especially if you have teenagers who are searching for their identity outside of the family. If your kids want to go somewhere that is not within your budget, tell them. Begin to plan ahead for day trips that may require reservations. Create a healthy balance of family and individual activities, down time, and white s p a c e on your calendar for spontaneity.

2. The day before and after your vacation, hire someone to come in and clean your house. You will be able to afford it with the money you save on air travel, hotel accommodations, and dining out.

3. Change the message on your answering machine and/or cell phone to reflect that you are on vacation. In it, give the date of your return and ask them to call you back, which will greatly reduce the number of messages. Use an "out of office" reply for responding to email. Give your contact information to one person at the office with the understanding that they will call you for emergencies only.

4. Decide if you want to have your mail delivered or withheld. It's easy to hold your mail by logging onto www.usps.com. Just click on "hold mail."

5. Give yourself some free time by hiring a babysitter for a block of time, or hire a teenager for the week to help out.

6. Take those day trips that you never have time for. Many of us live within driving distance of popular attractions that others have to travel by air to see.

7. If you like to putter around the house, clear out and organize those closets, drawers, and catchall rooms. Activities that restore order in our lives can be relaxing, accomplishing, and very liberating. Eliminate tolerations as you go (see chapter on *Tolerations*).

8. Treat yourself to a facial, haircut, pedicure, massage, or anything else that makes you feel totally pampered and nurtured.

9. Do things that you ordinarily wouldn't do. Take a one-day workshop. Browse your favorite bookstore or gift shop without any time restrictions. Send a handwritten letter. Go to a play, concert, or movie. Enjoy a long, decadent lunch with a friend at your favorite restaurant.

10. Change your routine. Sleep in. Go out for breakfast. If you feel like lying around in your pajamas all day, then do it.

11. Throw a potluck supper or barbecue. It's a great way to catch up with relatives and friends without having to do all of the work.

12. Revive your hobbies. They will nurture creativity and give you *s p a c e* to live more fully in the present moment.

*There are ways to be alone that,
while not as profound as meditation or hours spent in nature,
also offer enormous reward to the soul.
Being alone doing nothing is an art, and like all art
you need to practice it to reach your highest potential.
Do not stint. Do not consider it a waste of time.
Do not feel unworthy.
The self is sacred, both as individual
and as part of the flow of the universe in and out of time.*

– unknown

Energy leaks through the mouth by idle talk,
gossiping, censure, scandal mongering
and all sorts of useless worldly talks.
People do not understand the value
of energy. They waste it very carelessly.

– Swami Sivananda Saraswati

When all is said and done,
a lot more is said than done.

– Len Holts

VERBAL CLUTTER

If the thought of drawers filled to capacity, disorganized closets, and endless piles of paper drain your energy, how do you think verbal clutter feels to the body? Growing up in my home, dinner around our table of seven was like a cocktail party. Everyone talked at once; instead of negotiating, we argued. I learned how to interrupt, finish peoples' sentences, and dole out unsolicited advice. Needless to say, I had to practice a lot of undoing over the years.

As you move through your daily conversations with others, notice the amount of verbal clutter that you speak, read, or listen to on a daily basis. Keep in mind that less is more, actions speak louder than words, and there is tremendous power in silence.

Here are twelve examples of verbal clutter:

1. Expressing negative, critical, and/or judgmental words regarding yourself and others.

2. Avoid habitual interrupting and finishing people's sentences.

3. Giving too much information when answering a question.

4. Inability to receive graciously. Instead of simply saying thank you, you launch into a monologue about how you don't deserve or can't accept something.

5. Feeling the need to explain even when you don't want to.

6. Dominating conversations or droning on about your problems.

7. Apologizing about the same thing over and over again. If you really mean it, once is enough.

8. Talking incessantly. Buddha says, "Those who know are silent. Those who do not babble on forever."

9. Demonstrating grandiosity, making excuses, and dishonesty. This includes agreeing with someone when you don't.

10. Barraging people with questions to keep the focus on them because you feel uncomfortable.

11. Using offensive language and being loud.

12. Interjecting meaningless filler words in conversation, such as "ya know," "uh," "um," "really." When you talk to strangers, practice omitting these words from your language. Replace verbal clutter with a pause to allow your mind to catch up.

Clutter is the disease of American writing.
We are a society strangling in unnecessary words,
circular constructions, pompous frills
and meaningless jargon.

– William Zinsser

The tragedy of our time is that we are so eye centered, so appearance besotted.

– Jessamyn West

VISUAL CLUTTER

Imagine walking into your office and finding a messy desk, a trash can that hasn't been emptied, and stacks of stuff scattered all over the place. Most likely, instead of feeling inspired to work, you are suddenly tired and irritable. This happens because visual clutter disrupts the flow of energy.

Other drains include hard-to-navigate websites that contain too much information. Or, how about those retail stores, some of which are so jam packed with merchandise that it feels like a workout just to get through the racks of stuff?

One exception is Nordstrom with their legendary service, soft lighting, simple displays, and conscious utilization of s p a c e. They are creating an atmosphere that allows their customers to feel more relaxed and *want* to spend time there. Similarly, successful advertisers and retailers know that we are much more likely to notice a print ad with a lot of white s p a c e rather than one that is cluttered with too many words and pictures.

As a home stager, I encourage sellers to begin by reducing the amount of visual clutter. I want the buyer to walk into a room and have it look clean, peaceful, and spacious. Congestion becomes a distraction and the chances of them making an offer is less likely to happen. It's how the home makes them feel that will ultimately sell it.

Visual clutter also gets stored in our minds. One example would be the agony of witnessing violence to someone else, especially if it happened to us when we were little. This could also include visual memories that are tied to shame, guilt, and embarrassment.

To neutralize painful memories so that they no longer have control over you, read about *feeling into the core* on p. 183. This technique is a very effective way to clear visual clutter and create s p a c e for personal expansion.

Depending on our tolerance level and personality, visual clutter affects us differently. There are any number of reasons we choose to live with it, ranging from the excuse to stay disorganized to self-protection to distracting us from moving forward in our lives. But what most people aren't aware of is the subtle impact that visual clutter has on our mental and emotional attitude.

Living is easy with eyes closed...
  – from *Strawberry Fields Forever*
  by the Beatles

*It began with a life-or-death decision to remove
the Needle of False Security from my arm,
turn away from the Medusa of Routine,
part the Veil of Bogus Guarantees and
pass on into that vital place where,
regardless of the question,
all you have to say is yes.*

– Sol Luckman

*If you want the fruit from the tree,
you have to go out on a limb.*

– anonymous

YES

It was late one night during an insomniac bout of channel surfing when I stumbled on an old rerun of *The Michael Douglas Show*. The program, taped twenty years before in February of 1972 was, for this nostalgic soul, a treasure waiting to be found. No sooner had I tuned in, however, when the show went to a commercial break, leaving my mind to drift from one memory to another like a steady, gentle breeze.

Back then Mike, with his handsome good looks and mild manner, was the talk show darling of daytime television. During college, in a lounge down the hall, a small band of followers would cut class to gather, smoke cigarettes, and lust naughtily. Mike Douglas reminded me of my 7th grade art teacher, Mr. Keene, whose class I was taking when the news came over the P.A. system that President Kennedy had been assassinated. I remember staring at the clock on the wall while my fellow classmates bowed their heads in prayer. It was 1:10 p.m.

When the sound of Mike Douglas' voice filtered back into my consciousness, I looked at the ship's clock. It was 1:10 a.m. and, while much of the East Coast was sleeping, I was about to hit pay dirt. John Lennon and Yoko Ono were on, co-hosting the show.

I loved John Lennon. I loved him for his timeless "give peace a chance" lyrics. John was one of those rare, authentic people who lived by his own lights. Together, he and Yoko participated in the infamous "bed-in" on national television at the Amsterdam Hilton, affirming to his fans that life would never be dull as long as he was alive.

Now, as Douglas and his two co-hosts were bantering back and forth, John began to share the story of how he and Yoko met. In 1966, Yoko was exhibiting her artwork in a London gallery when Lennon casually dropped by. After the two were introduced, she handed him a card that said "breathe." John then noticed a short ladder that was leaning against a cubbyhole in the ceiling. Intrigued, he walked over and, looking up from the bottom rung, spotted a small-framed canvas.

"So," he told Mike Douglas in his charming British accent, "I decided to climb up."

There, at the top of the opening, he found a magnifying glass hanging next to the canvas where, in very small print, Yoko had printed one word - y e s. Before they broke for another commercial, Lennon shared with the television audience that y e s was a message for him to follow his heart.

I popped up off the sofa to make a cup of green tea, heating the water in the microwave so as not to miss even one second of the show. My timing was perfect. The tea was ready just as the next segment came on. Yoko sang a song that she had written, which I think had something to do with sisters. Then his last guest came on - a stark contrast to the Lennons - who reminded me of Fred Kaps, the magician who came on right after the Beatles' appearance on The Ed Sullivan show in 1964.

Before the show went off the air, Mike thanked the Lennons and invited them back. I heard two bells ring from the clock in the hallway and turned off the television. The mere touch of that remote button less than an hour ago had shifted the entire landscape of my evening.

In the quiet solitude of the night, I thought about John Lennon, the metaphor in the story and how his life might have been different had he chosen to walk around the ladder. By making the effort to climb the ladder into unknown territory, he not only found a sign that inspired him, but received a glimpse into Yoko Ono's world which produced an energetic match that lasted until his death in 1980.

For John Lennon, one small risk really paid off...

Freedom's just another word
for nothing left to lose.

– Kris Kristofferson

At the end of every road you meet yourself.

– S.N. Behrman

ZEE LAST PAGE

This photograph was taken in 1953 when I was two years old. I saw it for the first time at the age of thirty when my mother gave me a box of childhood memorabilia. At first glance, I thought is was my sister, Kristan.

About the Author

KATER LEATHERMAN'S self-taught careers span four decades and include painting houses on Nantucket Island, employing herself as a personal chef, working for a divorce lawyer, running her own catering business, and teaching people how to put together creative photo albums and scrapbooks.

Currently, she teaches yoga and is a professional organizer, budget redecorator and home stager. Kater's work has been published in *Glamour* magazine, *The Oakland Tribune, Bay Weekly,* and *Outlook By The Bay.* She leads declutter support groups and has a monthly column in *The Annapolis Capital* called *Kater on the Homefront.*